Inventory Optimization and Multi-Echelon Planning Software

Concepts Explained with Screen Shots and Examples from MEIO Applications

Shaun Snapp

Copyrighted Material

Inventory Optimization and Multi-Echelon Planning Software

Copyright © 2012 by SCM Focus Press

ALL RIGHTS RESERVED

No part of this publication may be reproduced, stored in a retrieval system or transmitted, in any form or by any means—electronic, mechanical, photocopying, recording or otherwise—without prior written permission, except for the inclusion of brief quotations in a review.

For information about this title or to order other books and/or electronic media, contact the publisher:

SCM Focus Press
PO Box 29502 #9059
Las Vegas, NV 89126-9502
http://www.scmfocus.com/scmfocuspress
408-657-0249

ISBN: 978-0-9837155-0-4

Printed in the United States of America

Cover and Interior design by: 1106 Design

Contents

CHAPTER 1:	Introduction	1
CHAPTER 2:	Where Inventory Optimization and Multi-Echelon Planning Fit within the Supply Chain Planning Footprint	7
CHAPTER 3:	Inventory Optimization Explained	15
CHAPTER 4:	Multi-Echelon Planning Explained	37
CHAPTER 5:	How Inventory Optimization and Multi-Echelon Work Together to Optimize the Supply Plan	65
CHAPTER 6:	MEIO Versus Cost Optimization	77
CHAPTER 7:	MEIO and Simulation	99
CHAPTER 8:	MEIO and Service Level Agreements	115
CHAPTER 9:	How MEIO is Different from APS and MRP/DRP	127
CHAPTER 10:	Conclusion	139
References		145
Vendor Acknowledgements and Profiles		149
Author Profile		151
Abbreviations		155
Links in the Book		157
Appendix A: MEIO Visibility and Analytics		161
Appendix B: The History of Development of MEIO Versus MRP/DRP		165
Index		175

CHAPTER 1
Introduction

Background and Motivation
Learning about inventory optimization and multi-echelon planning (MEIO) has been an interesting road for me. When I first implemented this type of application, I thought the functionality of MEIO was essentially similar to the advanced planning software I had been

implementing for years. Thanks to my own efforts to learn the technology, however, combined with the support of MEIO software vendors, I gradually learned that MEIO is not only different from the advanced planning methods in which I had previous experience, but also had a number of advantages. Once I understood MEIO, I appreciated how beneficial the technology could be. I began documenting aspects of MEIO, first in a blog on service parts planning and then later in a separate MEIO blog. This blog can be viewed at the link below:

http://www.scmfocus.com/inventoryoptimizationmultiechelon

As my writing about this topic progressed, I found that more people were reading the articles and I developed a number of relationships based on our common interest in MEIO. Furthermore, the increased use of MEIO terminology on projects, in conferences and in publications seemed to imply that MEIO was gaining broad popularity. However, I received the first inkling that the general acceptance of MEIO was going to be more effort than anticipated after the large consulting company I was working with fought me on the recommendation of MEIO for a client for whom I was confident MEIO would have been a perfect fit. I was given another rude awakening when I attended a supply chain conference and was surprised by the misuse of terminology relating to MEIO. I further began to notice that white papers written by consulting firms and vendors misrepresented the terminology surrounding MEIO with alarming frequency as they evidently viewed it as a yet another buzzword among many that they could use to sell work. The link below is to a blog that I wrote about the misuse of MEIO terminology by one firm.

http://www.scmfocus.com/inventoryoptimizationmultiechelon/2010/10/booz-allen-hamilton-misrepresents-inventory-optimization-in-white-papers/

I spoke with several MEIO vendors and they agreed with what I had observed. They reported that they were constantly involved in education on the basics of MEIO.

The Necessity of Good Information to Support Good Decisions
My conclusion, then, is that many, if not most, people who come across the terms "inventory optimization" and "multi-echelon" end up misinformed about what

these terms mean. Companies that don't understand MEIO cannot make good vendor-selection decisions and cannot at this stage rely on advice from consulting companies that work in supply chain planning—most of them also don't work in MEIO. These firms often have only a hazy understanding of MEIO themselves, or are more interested in promoting the established approaches for which they have trained resources ready to assign to projects. This is where the idea for this book began. I wanted to explain in lay terms what MEIO is, why works so differently, and the specific strengths that it brings to the table.

The underlying mathematics of MEIO are quite complex and beyond the grasp of most supply chain professionals. However, this advanced math is already encapsulated in MEIO applications, making it unnecessary for users to understand all the mathematics to gain the benefits from this technology. All that is required to use MEIO is to understand at a conceptual level how the technologies enable precise control over the supply plan. Once this is understood, the output of MEIO software is quite intuitive. Hands-on experience with the application—changing parameters and checking the resulting outcomes—is essential to get a deeper appreciation of how the application really works "under the covers."

Therefore, this book is designed for the layperson that needs to gain an understanding of MEIO. The book includes little math, and instead explains the technologies conceptually and relies heavily on graphics. For those who are interested in the underlying math, Craig C. Sherbrooke has written several books that cover the topic mathematically.

The Importance of Software Screenshots and Vendor Diversity

Unlike most books about software, this book showcases more than one vendor. Focusing an entire book on a single software application is beneficial for those that want to use solely the application in question. However, only the biggest vendors like Oracle and SAP tend to get books that showcase their applications, leaving out a lot of educational and interesting functionality that is distributed across other vendors. I prefer to use examples of software from multiple vendors to demonstrate concepts, meaning that I sometimes draw examples from multiple vendor applications. Using more than one vendor provides a much greater flexibility in this regard. However, it's also important for the reader to understand that I am completely independent from all the software companies whose products I cover. The specific application screen shots used in this book were selected because I found them to be good examples of functionality in an area, and they helped me demonstrate a concept.

I consult in some popular and well-known applications, and I've found that companies have often been given the wrong impression of an application's capabilities. As part of my consulting work, I am required to present the results of testing and research about various applications. The research may show that a well-known application is not able to perform some functionality well enough to be used by a company, and point to a lesser-known application where this functionality is easily performed. Because I am routinely in this situation, I am asked to provide evidence of various statements of the testing results within applications, and screen shots provide this necessary evidence.

Furthermore, some time ago it became a habit for me to include extensive screen shots in most of my project documentation. A screen shot does not, of course, guarantee that a particular functionality works, but it is the best that can be done in a document format. Everything in this book exists in one application or another, and nothing described in the book is hypothetical.

How Writing Bias is Controlled at SCM Focus and SCM Focus Press

Bias is a serious problem in the enterprise software field. Large vendors receive uncritical coverage of their products, and large consulting companies recommend the large vendors with the resources to hire and pay consultants rather than the vendors with the best software for the client's needs.

Just as in my consulting practice, I do not financially benefit from a company's decision to buy an application that I showcase. SCM Focus has the most stringent rules related to controlling bias and restricting commercial influence of any information provider in the space. These "writing rules" are expressed in the link below:

http://www.scmfocus.com/writing-rules/

If other information providers in this space followed these rules, I would be able to learn about software without being required to perform my own research and testing project on every topic.

Information about enterprise supply chain planning software can be found on the Internet, but it is primarily promotional or written at such a high level that none of the important details or limitations of the application are exposed; this is true of books as well. When only one enterprise software application is covered in a book, the application works perfectly; the application operates as expected, and there are no problems during the implementation to bring the application live. This is all quite amazing and quite different from my experience of implementing enterprise software. However, it is very difficult to make a living by providing objective information about enterprise supply chain software, especially as it means being critical at some time. I once remarked to a friend that SCM Focus had very little competition in providing unvarnished information on this software category, and he said, "Of course, there is no money in it."

Why Are There So Few Books on MEIO?

Something I noticed when doing research for this book is that there are few books distinctly on MEIO listed on Amazon.com. One book, *Inventory Optimization in SAP,* is actually misnamed, as it covers inventory management in the SAP Advanced Planner and Optimizer product, and not inventory optimization. In fact, as of the date this book was published, inventory optimization does not exist in any SAP product. *Inventory Optimization in SAP* is the highest listed book under the topic of inventory optimization on Amazon.com, and the book has nothing at all to do with inventory optimization. That in itself is indicative of the general level of knowledge on this issue. Another book listed is a user manual for an SAS inventory optimization product, and the final book I found was *Network Design and Inventory Optimization,* which is primarily focused on service parts planning. The books and articles on multi-echelon planning were either Sherbrooke's or primarily academic articles. With research, I found that no book specifically focused on MEIO *software*. However, software is the only way that the predominant number of supply chain professionals will ever interact with MEIO.

I felt certain that a book on inventory optimization and multi-echelon planning—particularly a plain-language book—was missing from the marketplace. I also felt that a book was required to explain MEIO in practical terms to business people. This is the book that you see before you. I have written this book so that any person with a reasonable understanding of supply planning should be able to understand MEIO conceptually. The focus is on how MEIO software works and can be used as a reference after the initial reading.

The SCM Focus Site

As I stated previously, I am also the author of the SCM Focus MEIO site (http://www.scmfocus.com/inventoryoptimizationmultiechelon). The site and this book share many concepts and graphics, and I have included in this book a number of links to the site. This is the most popular non-vendor-affiliated MEIO site on the Internet and is a part of the broader SCM Focus site (http://www.scmfocus.com), which covers a variety of supply chain software topics. If your interest in MEIO continues to grow, the site, to which articles are added regularly, is a complementary resource for you to investigate.

Who Is This Book For?

Early reviewers of this book described it as an effective primer for anyone looking to perform a MEIO software selection, anyone beginning a MEIO project at their company, or anyone who just wants to stay up to date on the state of the art in supply chain planning software. If you have any questions or comments on the book or the SCM Focus MEIO site, please email me at shaunsnapp@scmfocus.com.

Abbreviations

A listing of all abbreviations used in the book is provided at the end of the book.

CHAPTER 2

Where Inventory Optimization and Multi-Echelon Planning Fit within the Supply Chain Planning Footprint

Introduction

MEIO is an innovative use of two separate forms of optimization: inventory optimization and multi-echelon inventory optimization (but which I simply refer to as multi-echelon planning to reduce confusion). Each answers separate supply chain planning questions. Inventory optimization answers the question of how much to keep in inventory, while multi-echelon planning answers the question of where to keep inventory in the supply network. Unlike supply planning techniques that use sequential processing or calculation, MEIO calculates the service level impact of carrying one additional item at every product location combination and then sorts the list of options by their contribution to service levels and selects the best contributor.

The mathematics of inventory optimization and multi-echelon planning are combined to improve the inventory and service planning of the supply network; the graphic on the following page illustrates where they fit into the larger supply chain software context.

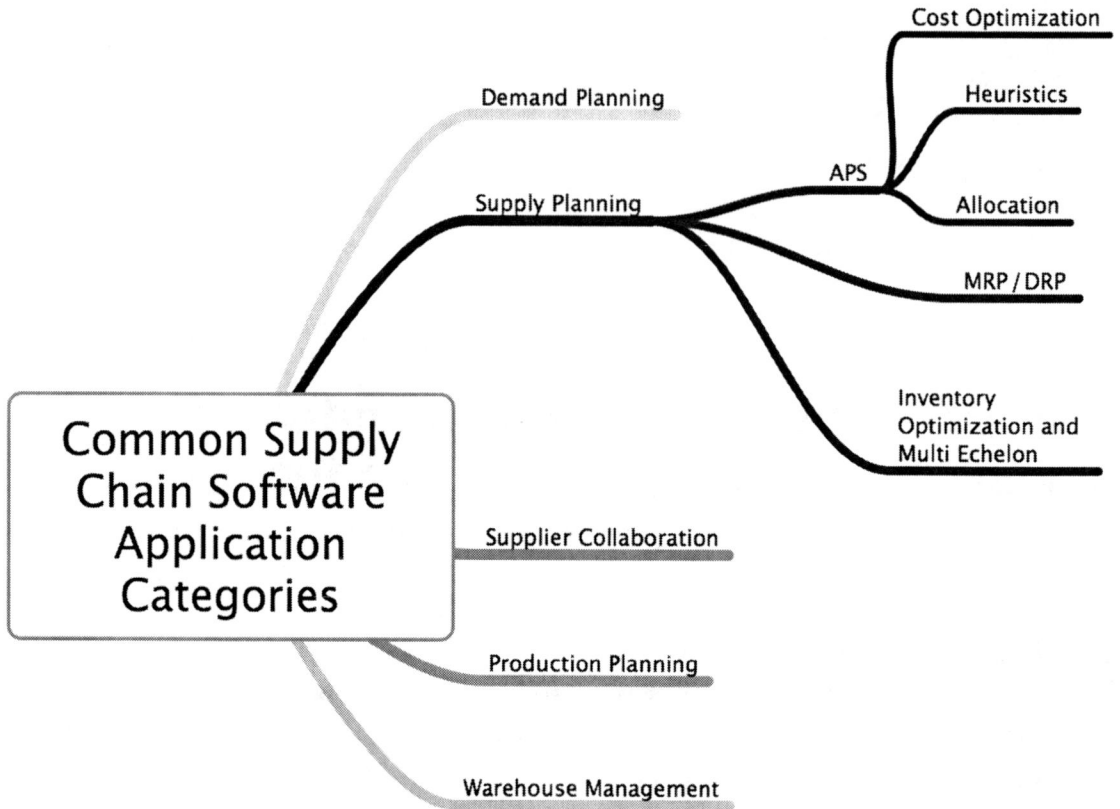

As you can see, MEIO is its own category of supply planning and is one of the three major methods of supply planning. MEIO is the most recently developed method and is also the least understood among supply chain professionals. As will be described in detail in this book, MEIO is founded on very different assumptions from the methods that preceded it.

What MEIO Applications Cover

Some MEIO applications such as SmartOps cover only supply planning, while others such as MCA Solutions and ToolsGroup perform both demand planning and supply planning. However, the fact that vendors may offer demand planning, even within the same application in which they offer supply planning, should not confuse the fact that MEIO mathematics is solely a method for supply planning. Because this is a point of confusion, I want to clarify the distinction here:

Mathematics that does anything with respect to inventory optimization and multi-echelon planning has nothing to do with the demand plan.

Understanding the Use of the Demand Plan Forecast with MEIO
All MEIO applications are able to use the customer's existing demand planning application's forecast. As a result, it is up to the vendor whether to add a demand planning module to their MEIO supply planning application. It is quite common for vendors that provide supply planning software to provide demand planning software as well, and this is as true of MEIO vendors as non-MEIO vendors. Doing so can offer some obvious benefits. For instance, MCA Solutions provides forecasting customized for service parts environments. Unlike MCA Solutions, ToolsGroup does not focus on a specialized industry segment, but has a strong forecasting application in addition to its MEIO application. Also, as will be discussed in Chapter 4: Multi-Echelon Planning Explained, where the forecast is applied is an important requirement for MEIO. However, none of these reasons change the fact that the mathematics for MEIO is centered in supply planning. For this reason, I will discuss supply planning exclusively in this book, even though a number of MEIO vendors offer both demand and supply planning functionality within the same MEIO product.

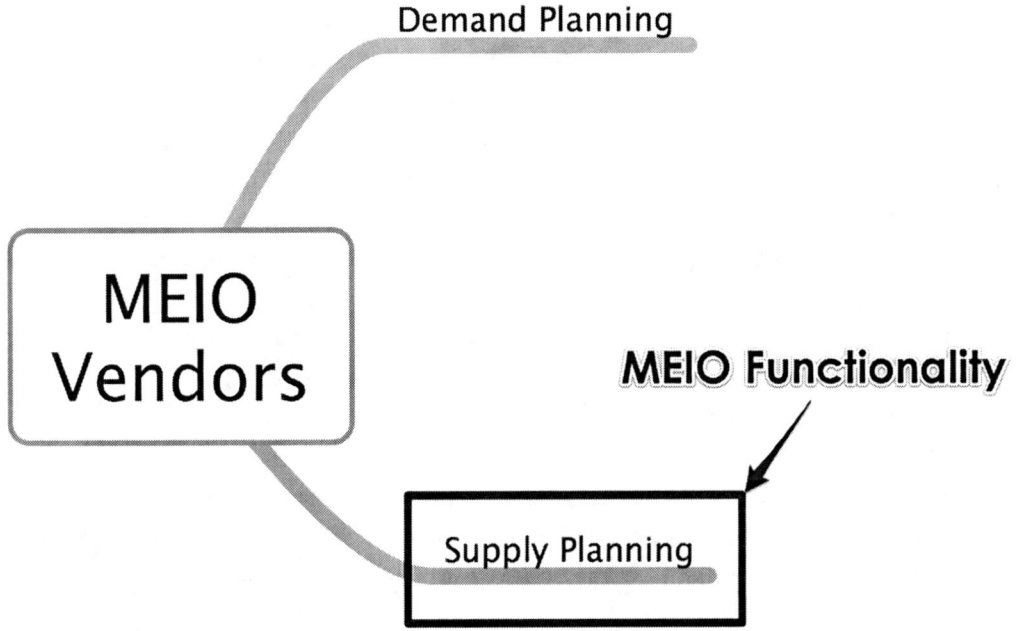

Optimization Customization

When a technology or method becomes popular in one area, it frequently migrates to other areas, often with mixed results. This is currently happening with "Lean," which has migrated from its origins on the manufacturing floor over to supply planning. (It has even found its way into construction where it is called "Lean Construction.") Interestingly, there is rarely any evidence provided that a particular method can or should be migrated to a new environment, but this rarely stands in way of such conversions. Therefore, if MEIO were to become more popular in supply planning, is it possible for it to branch out to manufacturing or even warehousing? While no one can predict the future, the applicability of MEIO is quite specific to supply planning. The introduction of optimization to the field of supply chain management, and the evolution of optimization away from one optimization method (cost optimization), has clearly demonstrated that optimization is most effective when it is customized for different supply chain domains (supply, production, transportation, etc.). This observation is not yet broadly understood, and is in fact rarely even brought up. However, in the future, I think it may come to be.

Analysis of the history of optimization in different supply chain domains shows that different supply chain domains have different ultimate goals and are best met with different objective functions. This is apparent in production planning and scheduling, where duration-based optimization provides several benefits over cost-based optimization, such as the fact that durations are simply much easier to agree upon than costs. The durations can be pulled from a master file, and can be used to populate the optimizer more accurately than costs could in a cost optimizer, the reason being that the data for durations is so much more reliable.

This has become quite obvious to me through interactions between multiple optimization vendors that specialize in different supply chain planning domains, but this topic is rarely written about, and any articles that are published tend to be in academic journals that business decision makers and consultants do not read. (Note: I performed a number of general web searches as well as academic article searches in Google Scholar and JUSTOR using a wide variety of terms related to comparative supply chain optimization methods. These searches returned no results that addressed this topic, other than an article on my own website SCM Focus.) The importance of optimization customization per supply chain domain is covered in the blog post found at the following link:

http://www.scmfocus.com/supplyplanning/2011/07/10/customizing-the-optimization-per-supply-chain-domain/

The majority of optimization application and method selection decisions are being made without knowledge of the importance of optimization specialization. This lack of awareness leads to the continual over-application of cost optimization in a wide variety of areas for which it is not the best approach.

In summary, my view is that inventory optimization is a particular method of optimization that has been perfected for supply networks. Because MEIO optimizers are customized for supply planning, MEIO is less likely to transfer well outside of the environment for which it was designed. MEIO is also one of several second-generation optimizers that are more customized for their domains.

Why Learn about MEIO?
MEIO is beneficial to understand because it is one of the major methods used in supply planning. It is the most appropriate method of supply planning if the goal of the company is to *minimize* the supply network inventory while *maximizing* the company's service level. As will be covered, MEIO offers a unique blend of advantages with respect to implementation and maintenance.

What Companies Stand to Gain the Most From MEIO?
Optimization generally tends to benefit situations that are more complex, and where a supply network is closer to capacity than under capacity. Supply networks that have more complexity—for example, more valid location-to-location combinations, more echelons (layers of parent-child relationships in the supply network), more SKUs, and more extensive service levels to meet—have more opportunities to benefit from MEIO than do less complex environments. Yet all but the smallest and simplest supply networks can in some way benefit from MEIO.

What is the State of MEIO Applications?

Nothing in this book is hypothetical. Everything that I will describe currently exists in a variety of forms within the software of different vendors. MEIO solutions are mature and have been tested at companies with very large volumes of data. They are ready to be implemented at companies of all sizes. After having personally integrated a MEIO system with an Enterprise Resource Planning (ERP) system, I can say that integrating systems of this type is a straightforward process and should certainly not dissuade companies from taking advantage of MEIO. Still, only a small percentage of companies that could benefit from MEIO have implemented it, and this is, in my opinion, due to the fact that many companies do not sufficiently understand MEIO. Therefore, education—rather than MEIO technology or integration limitations—is the biggest limiting factor for the MEIO software market.

The MEIO Data Flow

A good way to understand an application category is to look at the data that flows into it and the output produced by it. To this end, I have produced a MEIO data flow graphic.

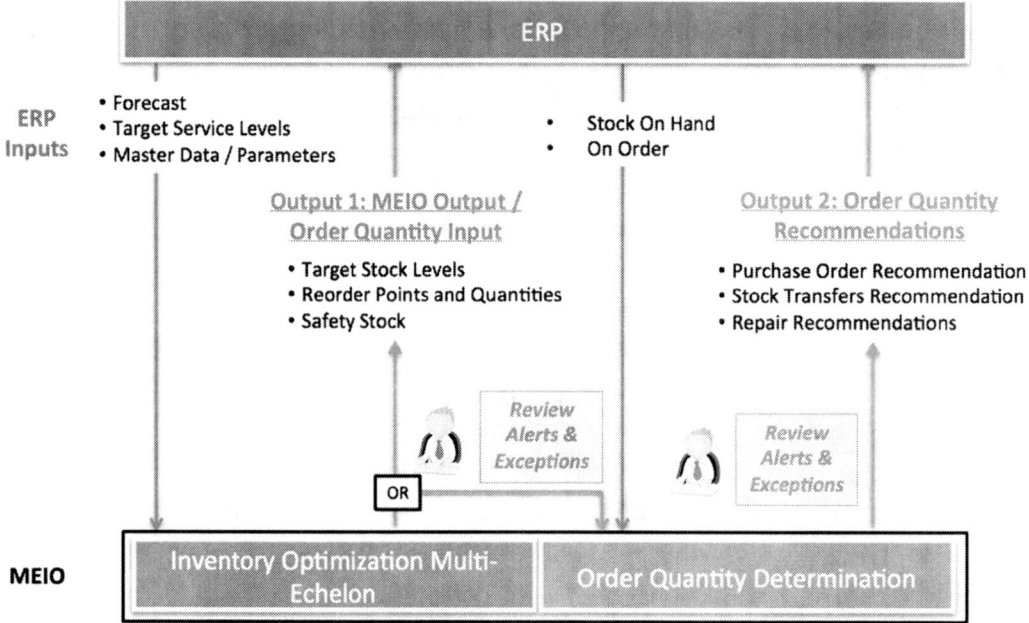

This graphic is a simplified version of a graphic that is used internally by MCA Solutions. It shows the data flow into and out of a MEIO supply planning system. It also shows that a flow can be within the MEIO application, or can flow directly from the inventory and multi-echelon optimization portion of the MEIO supply planning system to the ERP system.

This is important, because some MEIO applications only produce and send Output 1, while other MEIO applications internally process Output 1, and it is not until Output 3 is generated that the output is sent to the ERP system. Companies that use the MEIO system for order quantity determination and supply planning benefit from a better interface and a more sophisticated planning system than is available in ERP. For companies that only use Output 1, the MEIO application more or less runs in the background and planners require little training as they continue to use the ERP system for planning as they did prior to the MEIO implementation.

Conclusion

The combination of two supply planning technologies, MEIO is a major method of supply planning and as of 2012, understanding and acceptance of MEIO is still in the early stages. While MEIO is not right for every situation or every company, it has very differentiated benefits. Of all the supply planning methods, MEIO is in my view the most interesting to study because of what is actually going on "behind the scenes."

CHAPTER 3

Inventory Optimization Explained

Background

"Optimize" has become a popular business term that typically implies or describes some type of improvement or a better way of doing something. Its popularity is well known, but was further demonstrated when, at one supply chain conference, I observed that roughly one-third of all the presentations had the word "optimize" somewhere in their title or description.

Although the term "optimization" can be used to describe a general improvement in anything, "mathematical optimization" has a more specific meaning, and it's important to know what it is. Wikipedia defines mathematical optimization as follows:

> To choose the best element from some set of available alternatives. In the simplest case, this means solving problems in which one seeks to minimize or maximize a real function by systematically choosing the values of real or integer variables from within an allowed set.

Within mathematical optimization, there are more than twenty distinct types, one of which has inventory optimization as a sub-branch. The specific definition of inventory optimization differentiates it from all other types of optimization; however there is confusion in industry on what its definition is. Therefore, I developed a definition that has been well circulated. The link below offers a detailed definition of inventory optimization. This link can be useful if you need to send it to someone or bring it up during a meeting to get everyone on the same page.

    http://www.scmfocus.com/inventoryoptimizationmultiechelon/2010/04/inventory-optimization-definition/

Definition of Inventory Optimization

Inventory optimization is the derivation of stocking levels throughout the supply planning network based on service level targets. Inventory optimization answers the question of how much inventory should be carried, while—as I'll discuss later—multi-echelon answers the question of where in the supply network quantities should be carried. Unsurprisingly, these are the two most important questions in supply planning. Although all inventory optimization works this way, specifically how stocking levels are controlled by service levels depends on the individual approach of each particular MEIO vendor.

Inventory optimization software can be further described by where in the supply network service levels can be set. I have come to call this either the "inventory service level specificity" or the "service level hierarchy." This determines how the model is controlled and, therefore, it is important that companies understand what it is and how the control of service level differs among MEIO vendors—that is, where the implementing company wants to set the service level must match where the selected software allows the service level to be set. To read more about this topic see the post at the link below.

    http://www.scmfocus.com/inventoryoptimizationmultiechelon/2010/01/inventory-optimization-flexibility-and-the-service-level-hierarchy/

General Optimizers Solvers Versus Enterprise Optimization Solutions

Optimization software can be divided into two categories: enterprise software, which is the classification of software and the focus of this book, and off-the-shelf solvers. Enterprise software applies space optimization to supply planning, production planning, and occasionally transportation planning. Enterprise optimizers have the following attributes:

- They come with their own prebuilt optimization mathematics. The mathematics is based upon previously-published research, but is often adjusted by vendors based upon their own take on the math and their experience with the needs of different clients.

- They encapsulate or hide the mathematics within the overall application. Adjustments are not made to the mathematics of the optimizer but are made by changing the master data parameters.

- The optimizers within enterprise applications are just a part of the application, the applications being agglomerations of functionality and master data, user interface and so on.

- They are designed for a specific problem that has been found in many companies. For instance, a MEIO optimizer solves for a specific predefined problem.

General optimization solvers are essentially the opposite of the above attributes. You would purchase a general optimization solver when you want to create your own optimization mathematics or implement optimization mathematics from a published paper. They are stand-alone optimization solutions and tend to be used when the optimization problem is quite specific or for use as simulation environments. They actually can be used for any number of things, but they require resources with the appropriate advanced educations to build and run them properly. More on this is available at the post below:

http://www.scmfocus.com/supplychainsimulation/2011/10/12/understanding-the-difference-between-enterprise-optimizers-and-modeling-languages/

Examples of General Optimization Solvers

Anyone is free to create their own cost optimizer model by buying a general solver and then applying optimization algorithms from published papers. For instance, MathWorks makes a very popular mathematical modeling program called MATLAB that has found wide application in academics. MATLAB has two separate optimization plug-ins for its popular mathematical and matrix processing development environment.

Accelerating the pace of engineering and science

Products & Services   Solutions   Academia   Support   User Community   Company

Product Overview
- Description
- Function List
- Demos and Webinars
- Related Products
- System Requirements
- Latest Features

Support & Training
- Product Support
- Documentation
- Downloads & Trials

Other Resources
- Technical Literature
- User Stories

Optimization Toolbox
Solve standard and large-scale optimization problems

Optimization Toolbox™ provides widely used algorithms for standard and large-scale optimization. These algorithms solve constrained and unconstrained continuous and discrete problems. The toolbox includes functions for linear programming, quadratic programming, binary integer programming, nonlinear optimization, nonlinear least squares, systems of nonlinear equations, and multiobjective optimization. You can use them to find optimal solutions, perform tradeoff analyses, balance multiple design alternatives, and incorporate optimization methods into algorithms and models.

Inventory Optimization Explained

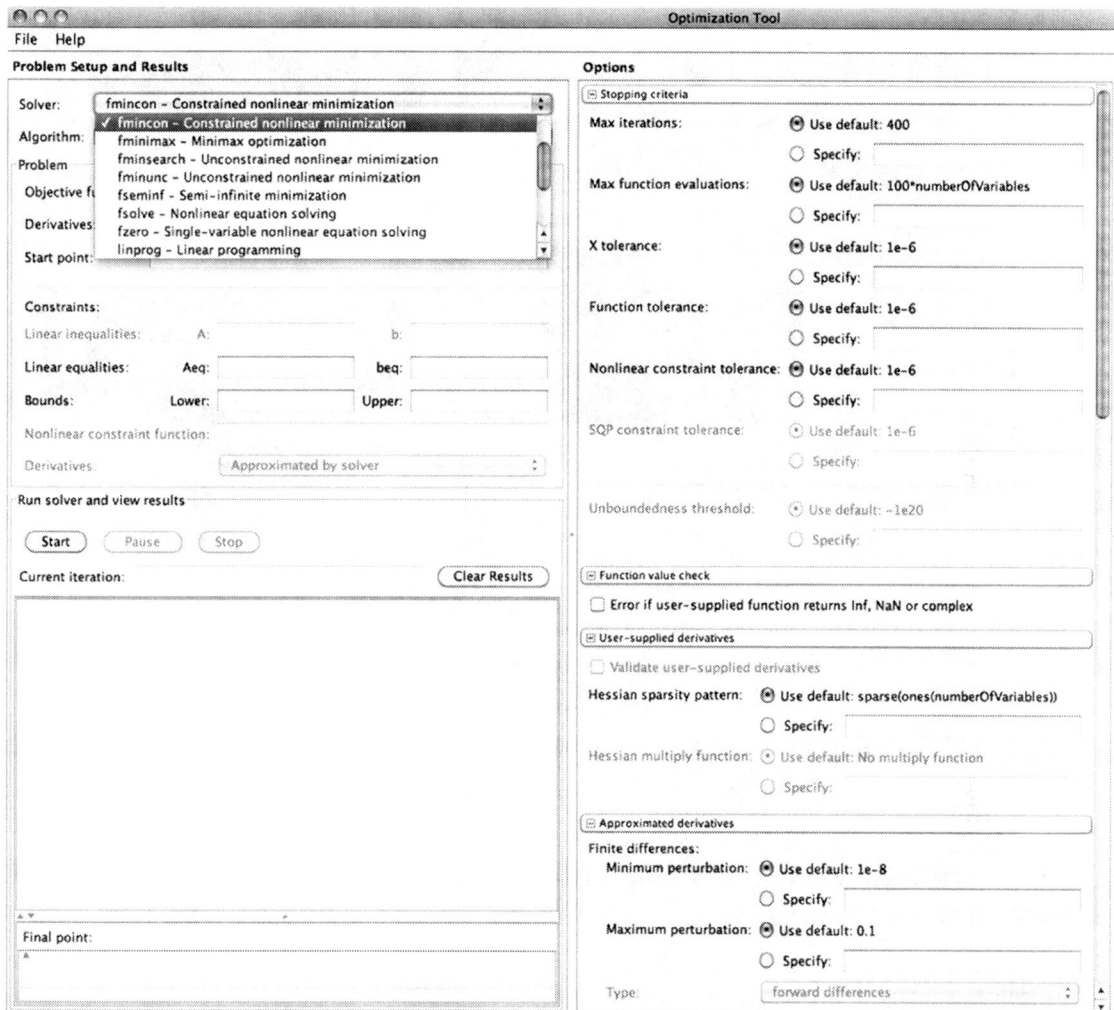

MATLAB offers a number of different optimizer categories to choose from. In addition to choosing the category, the mathematics and the conditions of the optimization must be entered into the application.

MATLAB also can be connected to a third party external optimizer, called CPLEX. CPLEX is a very popular and sophisticated optimizer that is at the heart of many enterprise optimization products.

In addition to MATLAB and CPLEX there are many other general solvers, both proprietary and open source. The Optimization Software Guide covers seventy-five different software packages and libraries. In fact, most enterprise vendors buy a general optimization solver and build their application around it so that the most typical design looks like the graphic shown on the next page.

Both the MATLAB's optimizer and CPLEX are general optimization solvers; that is, they can be used to optimize any situation for which there are parameters and an objective function (i.e., the goal of the optimization). These general solvers can solve for any objective function that is placed into the optimizer. Therefore, it is the mathematics used that determines the type of optimization to be performed. With the right resources, a full supply chain optimization application could be developed with any of these general optimization solvers, in addition to many others by a company desiring to implement an optimization system. However, it is rarely done due to the effort involved and the fact that software vendors are already offering products that encapsulate the solver along with a user interface and additional coding to make the optimizers solve a particular problem. This is consistent with the trend in the past several decades of companies purchasing enterprise software rather than building their own software from scratch or from components.

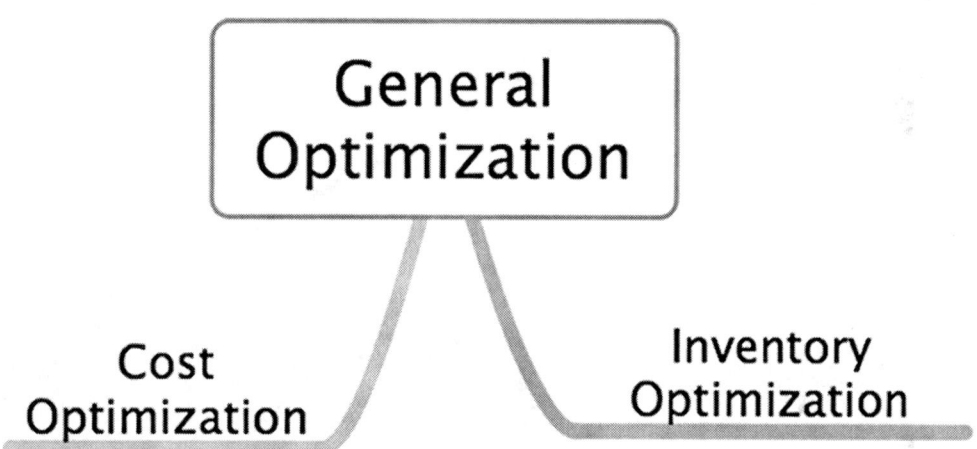

Dynamic Safety Stock

Any ERP system can calculate safety stock dynamically. Alternatively, safety stock can be entered manually as a hard-coded value or calculated externally by a variety of methods, including MEIO. (In fact, one popular method of using SmartOps is to export the safety stock calculated in SmartOps to the safety stock field in SAP ERP.) MEIO applications also have dynamic safety stock functionality; however, this is separate from inventory optimization. The safety stock is simply calculated based upon MEIO-derived initial stocking levels. Inventory optimization does not optimize the safety stock, but optimizes what MCA Solutions has coined the "target stocking level" (TSL), and does so for the entire supply network. Safety stock, on the other hand, is calculated independently at each location product combination. Safety stock is only a subcomponent of the TSL. The main functionality in MEIO goes toward calculation of the initial stocking level (ISL). It is from the ISL that the safety stock is derived.[1] By combining the ISL and the safety stock the TSL is derived. The relationship is as follows:

TSL = ISL + Safety Stock
See the graphic and formula here:

http://www.scmfocus.com/meiobook/files/2010/10/TSL_or_SS.jpg.

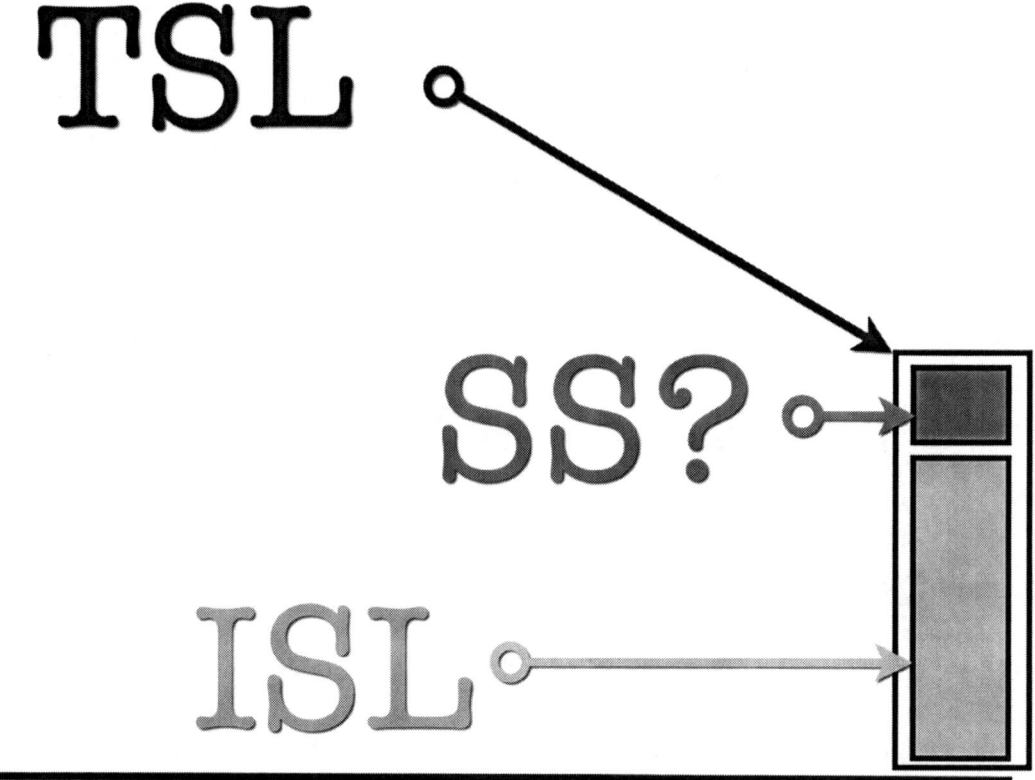

Therefore, the best way of thinking of TSL is as the total stock target at a location product combination. Safety stock, on the other hand, is simply the specialized subcomponent of the TSL quantity that accounts for the variability

---

[1] This is generally how the safety stock for MEIO applications is computed. However, different vendors have different ways of doing this and some offer multiple ways of calculating safety stock.

in supply and demand. Safety stock is represented conceptually by the following formula:

$$\text{Safety Stock} = (\text{ISL} \times \text{Supply Variability}) + (\text{ISL} \times \text{Demand Variability})$$

What It Means When One Says That "Safety Stock is Optimized"

Safety stock calculated with a MEIO application will be lower than the safety stock calculated by any other supply planning method. However, this is not due to MEIO's inventory optimization functionality, but rather to its multi-echelon functionality. Multi-echelon functionality can both see and interpret the relationships between locations that non-multi-echelon systems cannot. This is discussed in detail in Chapter 4: "Multi-echelon Planning Explained." Therefore, while it is true to say that safety stock is optimized by MEIO applications, the way it accomplishes this is a bit circuitous. Explaining this fact and validating the understanding of it is something that is integral to the success of MEIO projects, because implementing MEIO is, as with other supply planning methods, about more than setting up the system and ensuring it works properly. It is also about educating the users of the system so that they can make sense of the results. I have witnessed several projects where MEIO has either not been properly explained or the knowledge provided was not accepted and this invariably leads to ineffective use of the MEIO planning output. When this understanding has not been socialized within the company, planners and higher-ups will view the recommendations created by the MEIO application as suspect. This typically leads to system output being overwritten manually, an action that can be initiated directly by planners, or by supply-chain directors or vice presidents.

  Implementation

Safety Stock and Facility Capacity

Safety stock is only one output of MEIO software and its importance is frequently overestimated in the overall scheme of things with respect to the MEIO's output. However, when a company is constrained in its facility capacity, aggregate safety stock at a location takes on a special importance because the company cannot hold the safety stock calculated by the system. Often this is interpreted as something the system should manage; however, I don't think that this interpretation is correct. In fact, this should always be a short-term situation, because a reduction of the safety stock from the recommended quantity generated by the MEIO software will mean stocking-out customers in conditions of either negative supply or positive demand variance.

I have occasionally run across companies that want the safety stock to be restricted by facility capacity. They try it for a few weeks after a go-live and invariably turn the capacity constraint off. This is not a good practice and many of the planning systems that I am familiar with do not do this, but several do.

There are a number of alternative methods for dealing with this problem. Rather than place this complexity at the doorstep of supply planning, other solutions include acquiring more space (with dedicated facilities or third-party warehousing) or cutting the less profitable items from the database. Within supply planning, existing space can be used more effectively by running a procedure called redeployment, where stock already in the supply network is moved to new locations where it has a higher likelihood of being consumed. (Unfortunately, redeployment is not standard functionality in all supply planning applications, but it is a main MEIO competency.) Redeployment is covered in Chapter 5: "How Inventory Optimization and Multi-echelon Work Together to Optimize the Supply Plan." Through simulation, optimizers of any type—including MIEO—can be used to support these strategic decisions. This will be discussed further along in this chapter.

Understanding the General Relationship between Service Level and Inventory

The relationship between inventory and service levels is non-linear; higher and higher service levels require disproportionate increases in inventory to support them. The closer service levels come to one hundred percent, the more extreme the costs become. This relationship is one of the best-documented relationships in supply-chain management and is described by the graphic below.

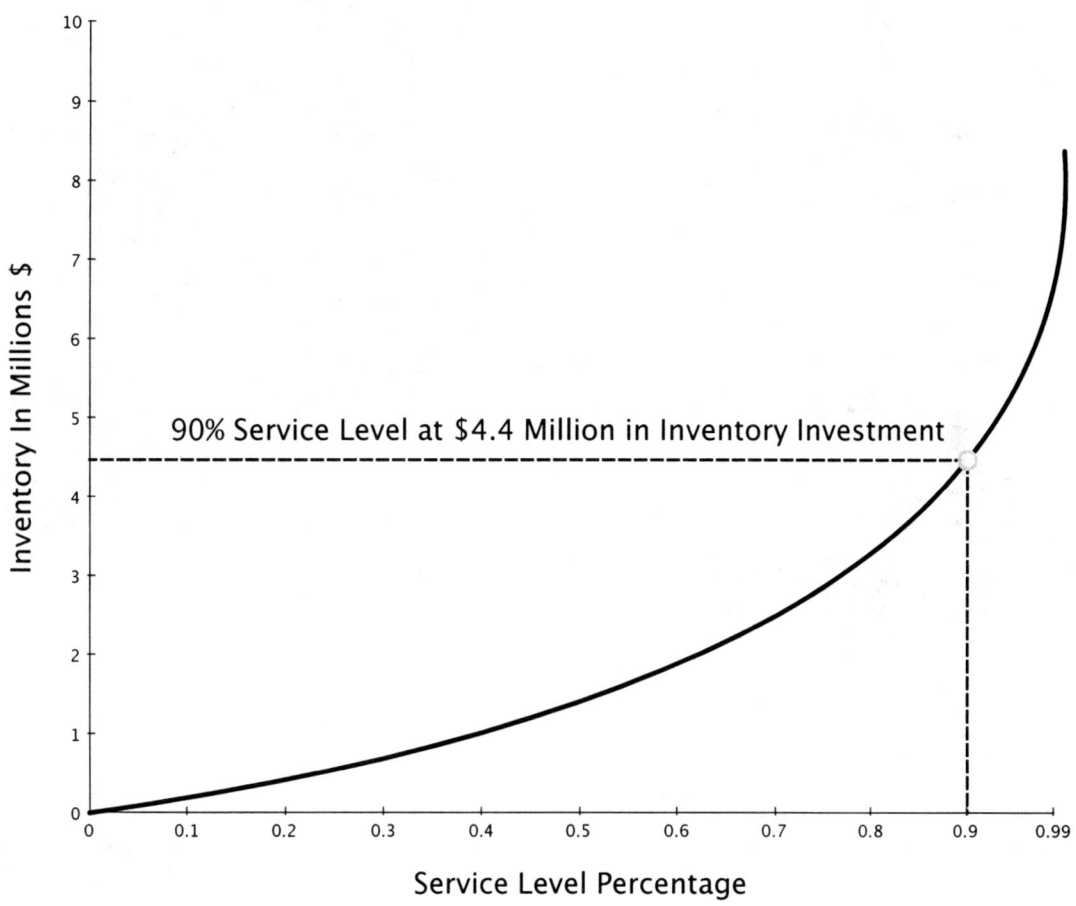

This graphic has been seen at one time or another by most supply chain professionals, and it demonstrates the fact that companies must decide what levels of service they can afford and, most importantly, what levels of service their customers are willing to pay for.

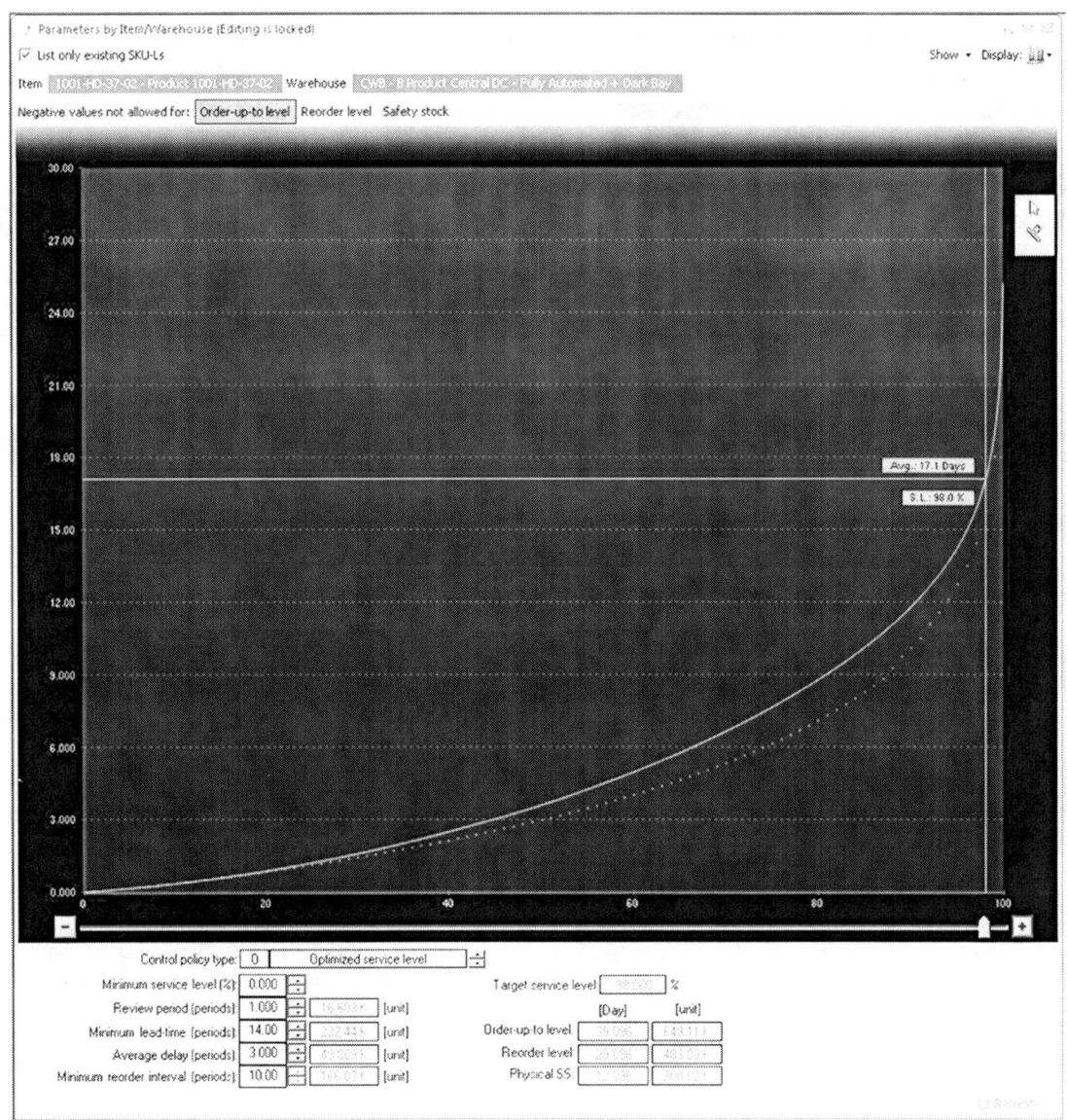

ToolsGroup has this curve built into their application. As you can see, their graph shows the same relationship as the graph on the previous page. Notice that there is a slider at the bottom of the ToolsGroup application view. This allows the user to see what the resulting inventory would be for different system-wide service levels. (A number of other parameters can be changed, as well as observed, from below the main graphic.)

It is impressive—considering all of the calculations that the ToolsGroup application has to perform in order to generate this graph—how easily the graph can be adjusted by simply moving the slider along the bottom. Behind the scenes, there is a fully configured model of the supply chain. This is supply chain simulation in a very easy-to-use form. This particular view is so useful that ToolsGroup is not the only MEIO vendor that has it. Below is the Inventory Optimization Efficient Frontier Analysis screen from Logility.

EFFICIENT FRONTIER ANALYSIS

Efficient Frontier Analysis displays the service vs. inventory trade-off curve for the supply chain model, and plots baseline performance as a point relative to that curve. Inventory metrics are calculated for the optimal inventory policy as service levels vary across the specified range for all demand stages in the supply chain, while the baseline point is to be entered from pre-implementation measurements.

Efficient Frontier Analysis: SP Product (Baseline)

1. Specify inventory measure: Total Inventory Investment
   Current Model Value: $4,015,662

2. Enter baseline (pre-implementation) value for measure: $5000000

3. Enter baseline (pre-implementation) effective service level: 96 %

4. Specify range of service levels to display:
   Minimum   95 %
   Maximum   99.99 %

5. Enter the number of points in the input range at which to measure the output: (Max = 100)   10

[Submit]

SmartOps also has a simulation view that shows the relationship between service level and costs. All of these applications provide a capability that companies implementing MEIO have not had before.

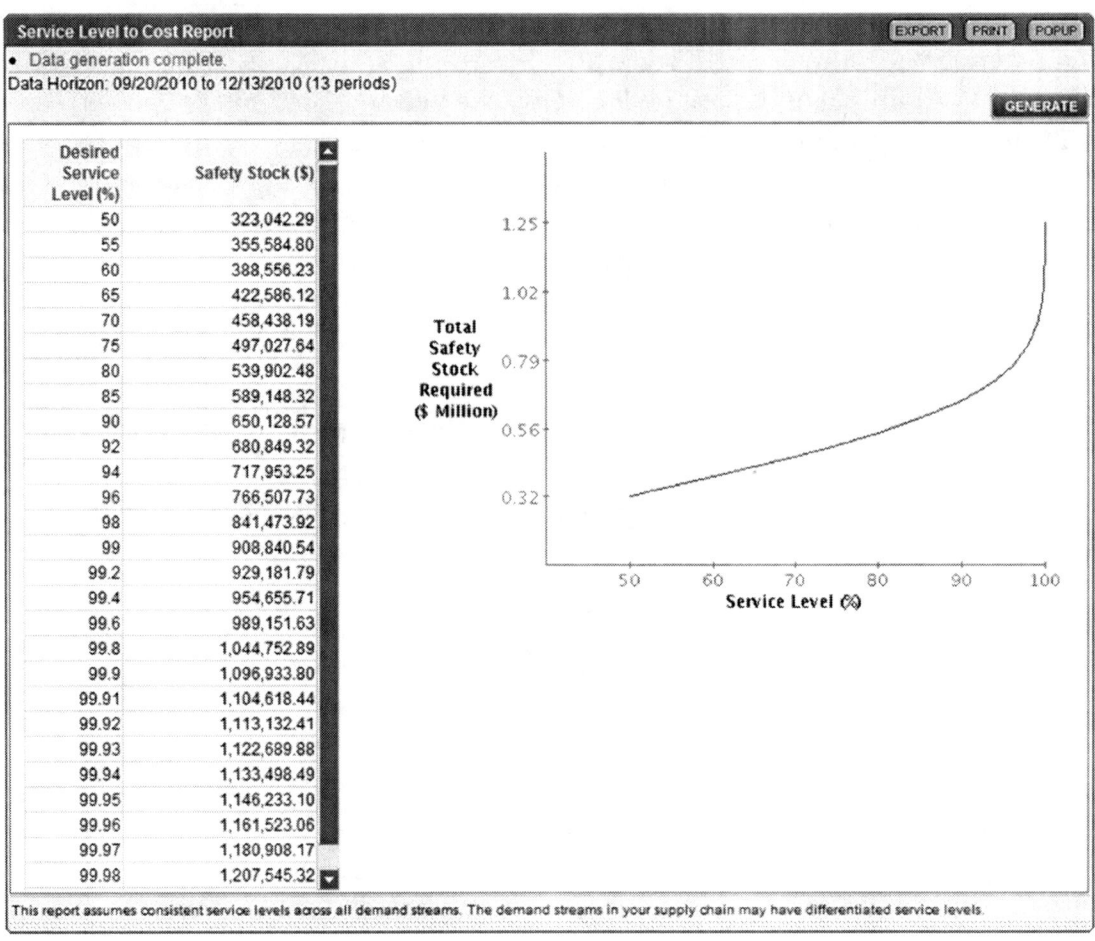

Interestingly, even though the service level to cost relationship is understood and settled among academics, MEIO software vendors and anyone with the mathematical understanding to prove the relationship, the lesson to be taken from this relationship does not resonate with the majority of supply chain executives. Decades after the service-level-to-inventory relationship has already been demonstrated, companies continue to hold unrealistic service level targets as correct. How do these companies continually meet unrealistic service level objectives if these objectives mathematically cannot be met with anything approaching reasonable inventory levels? The answer is simple: They don't actually meet them in reality. Most companies are able to meet their service level targets "on paper" using various methods that amount to inaccurate accounting for the service levels, but in reality they do not meet the targets. In my work I frequently comment that the service level targets that companies declare openly are either impossible to meet or would cost so much money to meet that their policy would put the company out of business. They often ask me how I can say this as I have only been at the company for a short time. My answer is the mathematical relationship, as is shown again below.

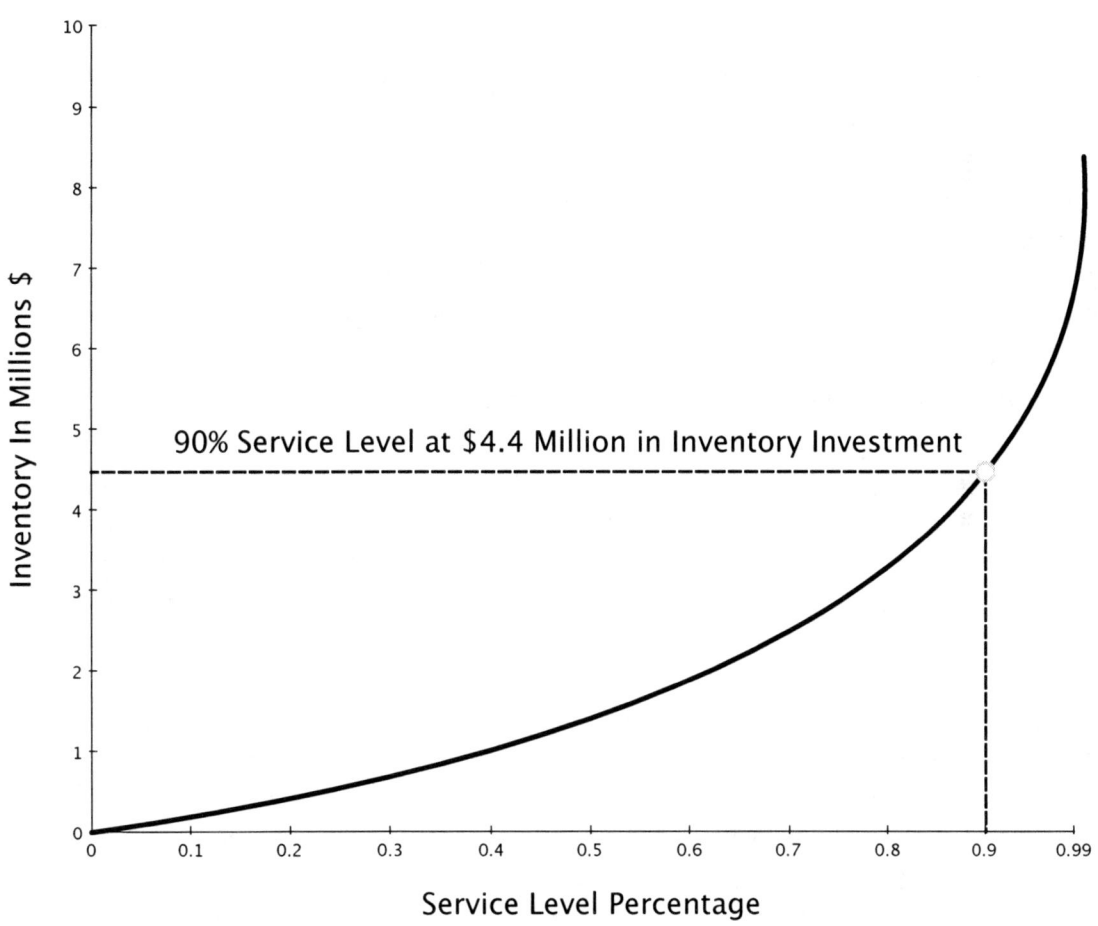

Conversations which attempt to get a company to set more reasonable goals can quickly devolve into a discussion over the importance of customer service to the company, as if the consensus on the mathematical relationship between service level and inventory levels is simply not convincing. It is also curious how many companies think that very high service levels are what distinguish them from the competition. However, if every company thinks that service levels are what differentiate them from the competition, then this obviously can't be the case. In addition, when overall service levels are analyzed, actual service levels turn out to be much lower than the estimates. Dr. Calvin Lee, in his paper on Demand Chain Optimization, states that:

> Studies have shown that 8.3 percent of shoppers on average will fail to find their product in stock. These stock-outs represent 6.5 percent of all retail sales.

Based on these studies, the service level would be either 91.7 percent or 93.5 percent depending upon whether the service level is measured at the individual demand, or the total of all units unfulfilled, divided by total units actually sold. This is a far cry from the 98, 99 and 99.5 percent that clients declare to me as their achieved service levels. Dr. Lee goes on to say essentially the same thing that I have found when I consult with companies on this topic:

> Compounding the problem, companies often assign target service goals based upon arbitrary judgments or by simply following the historical tradition, and they fail to carefully analyze the relationship between the customer service target level and the cost of excessive stock versus shortfall.

However, the story is actually worse than decision makers picking excessive service levels. Companies can also behave schizophrenically when it comes to the rising and falling importance of service level objectives over time. This is a well-known phenomenon, which I have observed at many clients, and is supported in the supply chain management literature. George Plossl has the following to say on this topic:

> The absence of intelligent policies relating to inventory levels also leads to a panic reaction to overweight inventories in times of falling business activity. The usual reaction is to issue a decree that inventories must be cut by some specific amount, without regard to the requirements of the

business and without full realization of the impact such cuts may have on customer service, costs and employment levels. Not only is customer service hurt, but also production rate changes caused initially by falling demand are amplified greatly by untimely and excessive inventory reductions. The reverse sequence occurs when business picks up again and crash programs are initiated to rebuild depleted inventories. Poor inventory management and production planning aggravate the effects of the business cycle. Modern society, as well as professional management should expect and demand better performance.

Depending upon the financial ups and downs of the company and the person setting the policy, the focus may be on inventory reduction during some periods, and at other times service levels become more highly prized. This leads back to the central concept and the main point of the next section: A service level that is not firmly established and supported by a mathematical linkage to how the company benefits is more likely to vacillate based upon external factors.

Control Over Service Levels

One of the major differences between MEIO and MRP, DRP and APS systems for supply planning is that MEIO has very direct control over service levels. In all other supply planning methods, the only direct control over service levels is the dynamic safety stock calculation. This can only be calculated locally (at one particular product-location combination) and is only for a portion of the TSL. MEIO has the ability to move the entire planned system-wide inventory up or down, much like the water level in a fish tank, and can do so very precisely depending upon the service level selected. This offers the supply planner unparalleled simulation capabilities, allowing him or her to fine-tune the supply plan and to do so quickly.

Safety Stock or Target Stocking Level Optimization?

Inventory optimization is sometimes confused for safety stock planning, but they are not the same thing. Many people who work in supply chain management are overly focused on safety stock to the detriment of understanding the total stock level. This became very apparent to me during a variety of meetings and discussions. In fact, in supply chain projects meetings, it is quite common to hear the term "safety stock" used reflexively in situations where it does not apply, leading me to conclude that the distinction between safety stock and other forms of stock is not broadly understood. This is strange, because it's a very simple concept. In addition, it is much less common to hear the terms "cycle stock" or "total stocking level," even though these are equally important concepts but also not understood. It is also not unusual to hear the term "safety stock optimization," and in fact, this term is also used by at least one MEIO vendor.

In my view, the reason that planners and other supply chain planning professionals tend to focus on safety stock is not because of formal training or reading about the topic, but because ***it is one of the few inventory values easily altered*** in all on-MEIO systems. Absent a foundational understanding of the topic, people have a strong tendency to base their views on what ***should*** be controlled because they ***can*** control it. This is reminiscent of the story about the man who, one night, is looking in the street for his keys. When asked where he lost them, he says, "On the other side of the street." He is looking on the wrong side of the street because "the light is better over here." In the same way, even though safety stock is not a good inventory value to adjust manually, it is frequently adjusted simply because it's a convenient way of controlling the stock level within many systems. This of course causes problems, as safety stock is simply the portion of overall stock allocated specifically to variability. In actual fact, stock levels should not be controlled by manually adjusting the safety stock. Instead safety stock should be dynamically calculated and automated, and only change as a result of changes in the variability of supply or demand. When this is done it is called "dynamic safety stock," and this functionality is now common in both ERP and APS systems, although surprisingly, not that frequently used.

More on why safety stock is not the focus of inventory optimization is available at the link below.

> http://www.scmfocus.com/inventoryoptimizationmultiechelon/2011/03/why-safety-stock-is-not-the-focus-of-inventory-optimization/

Segmentation or Inventory Optimization?

Segmentation is a method of selecting portions of the product database and applying changes to its control parameters. For instance, one could select all SKU locations that are above a certain number of inventory turns per year and apply one economic order quantity to them. This is a planning parameter. All the MEIO vendors have these types of parameters, as does MRP and every other supply planning software category. However, MEIO software does not segment the product database while applying ordering parameters to them. MEIO functionality and segmentation functionality are independent from one another. Segmentation functionality can be applied to any supply planning method (and in fact to other domains in supply chain planning such as production planning).

Segmentation capability is quite valuable because it allows planners to more effectively control the behavior of their products. It is a very direct method of filtering and control and, thus, has a higher likelihood of being carried out in actual practice than other methods of segmentation. This type of software combines aspects of master data management, supply planning, and reporting. In fact, some of the strongest supply planning reporting capabilities I have seen are with segmentation vendors; it can be justified as a replacement, at least partially, of the reporting and master data maintenance applications that the company is currently using.

Viewing Segmentation Software as Distinct from MEIO Software

Popularizing a new software category so that it is understood in the minds of corporate buyers is time consuming and expensive. However, it is ultimately necessary if the software is to become selected and implemented correctly. I hope to see a time when MEIO and segmentation are seen as the two separate categories of supply planning software that they indeed are. Using both systems would be paramount to purchasing and configuring two systems that have some areas of overlap.

For a number of years now, I have advised clients to stop thinking in terms of a single solution for supply planning and to entertain more than one supply planning solution—including external simulation tools and general optimization solvers—that can enhance their company's capabilities and meet more requirements that any one tool can, even with expensive enhancements. It is an uphill battle because the large consulting companies promote the mindset that all of the supply planning needs of a company can, and should, be met by a single application model. Financial incentives have blinded large consulting companies to better ways of doing things, and in the area of the solution ecology, I find that most of the major consulting companies simply have too many conflicts of interest for their views to be taken seriously. If an expert or resource is paid to think something, then it's logical to remove this opinion from consideration. To get an understanding of how deep these conflicts go, see the article below:

http://www.scmfocus.com/enterprisesoftwarepolicy/2012/01/27/how-common-is-it-for-sap-to-take-intellectual-property-from-partners/

To read more about segmentation versus inventory optimization, see the post below:

http://www.scmfocus.com/inventoryoptimizationmultiechelon/2010/11/segmentation-vs-inventory-optimization/

Conclusion

Inventory optimization is a subset of mathematical optimization. A solver is what computes the inventory optimization and the multi-echelon planning mathematics. The mathematics categorizes the optimizer. Inventory optimization and multi-echelon planning are customized forms of optimization specifically designed around the needs of supply planning. Among differences in their design approaches to solve the same problem, MEIO vendors differ substantially in terms of where the service level can be set in their applications.

Inventory optimization does not optimize the safety stock in the system, but optimizes the target stocking level at each product location based on a service level that can be set in a variety of locations. However, because safety stock is based on the initial stocking level, MEIO has the ability to calculate more efficient and often lower safety stock based on its more sophisticated modeling of the probable interactions of the locations in the supply network.

Inventory optimization is effective for supply planning because it is customized for the most important business goal of many, although certainly not all, supply planning organizations: the minimization of inventory at any service level. One of MEIO's major features is the control it gives planners and organizations over service levels. Highlighting their flexibility, MEIO applications can also start from an inventory goal and work toward the service level. MEIO software can demonstrate the relationship of every possible combination of service levels versus inventory investment and can recreate the relationship based on SKU level modeling. This capability replicates the inventory-to-service-levels graphic that is familiar to most supply chain professionals, and does so in a way that is very precisely based upon the company's real data, making MEIO applications very powerful for simulation. In fact, several MEIO applications allow for simulation by planners and do not require any special set-up.

CHAPTER 4

Multi-Echelon Planning Explained

Background

Multi-echelon planning represents the "ME" in the MEIO acronym. However, the term is used much less frequently than inventory optimization. Interestingly, multi-echelon planning was researched earlier than inventory optimization; the first multi-echelon planning research paper was published in 1958, while inventory optimization was not commonly written about until the 1970s. The logic to determine stocking decisions as presented in the first paper on multi-echelon planning, was not service level (inventory optimization) but rather a cost function with different stock-out costs per echelon. It was not until several years later, in 1976, that multi-echelon planning and inventory optimization mathematics were combined.

The term "echelon" is generally understood as multiple levels in the hierarchy of the supply network. However this definition requires explanation for those who are unfamiliar with the term. Moving stock between predefined parent and child locations in a supply network is called "deployment." In deployment, specific parent locations supply specific child locations. These locations can be called many things and companies typically assign slightly different names to locations that have the same function. Plants are often designated as the first parent echelon. Plants then feed depots or regional distribution centers. These locations, which are children to the plants, are themselves parents to the distribution centers. The assignment between parent and child locations—the valid location-to-location combinations in the supply network—is held in a table in the supply planning application. Each specialized layer is known as an "echelon."

There can be any number of echelons in a supply network. The number of echelons vary by company size and industry. For instance, a finished goods distributor that does no manufacturing would tend to have fewer echelons. A company that both manufacturers and services their product would have more.

The term "echelon" first appeared in published form in a 1958 paper by A.J. Clark, who explained the reason behind selecting this complicated way of saying "layer" or "level."

> The word 'echelon' is used rather than 'level' to avoid confusion with stock levels, rather than 'stage'—although the word has been used in this context—because 'multi-stage problems' has recently been used to designate problems in which time is divided into discrete decision intervals or stages.

The number of Google searches for these terms provides a good understanding of how frequently people are thinking about or researching them. According to Google, there were, in one month, 6,600 searches globally for "inventory optimization" but only 2,400 searches for "multi-echelon." One clear reason for inventory optimization's popularity is that it has been used much more frequently in promotional literature. While most supply chain professionals have an idea that inventory optimization is connected to service level planning, it's rare that I run into people other than MEIO vendors who understand the definition of multi-echelon planning.

The Questions that Each Term Answers
Inventory optimization and multi-echelon planning answer different questions regarding the supply plan, but one is not more important than the other. Together, they answer the two most important questions in supply planning:

1. How much should be carried? (Answered by inventory optimization)

2. Where in the supply network should quantities be carried? (Answered by multi-echelon planning)

Inventory optimization and multi-echelon planning work in conjunction with each other to place the optimal quantities at the optimal supply network location based on the forecast. How they work together is both important and quite interesting and is the topic of Chapter 5: "How Inventory Optimization and Multi-Echelon Work Together to Optimize the Supply Plan." A much less popular topic than inventory optimization in discussions about supply chains, multi-echelon functionality often does not get its fair share of attention, and discussions of MEIO tend to focus more on the service level benefits than on the positioning benefits of MEIO applications. This chapter will explain why multi-echelon is such an important capability for supply chain organizations to have.

Multi-Echelon Planning Defined
"Multi-echelon inventory optimization" is the official full technical name of what I refer to as either "multi-echelon" or "multi-echelon planning," and is often shortened to differentiate it from inventory optimization. Its full name is also quite a mouthful, so it certainly makes sense to use a shorter term. Multi-echelon planning is functionality that allows users to plan their supply network in a specific way—a way that changes the standard assumptions about the relationship between locations.

Unlike earlier methods of supply planning (which assume location independence), multi-echelon software assumes that the various locations in the supply network are *interdependent*—and it has the mathematics to treat them as such.

In multi-echelon planning, the stocking at a parent location affects the stocking decision and service level at the child location—a simple thing to say, but with huge implications. Other supply planning approaches do not work in this manner as they treat each location as independent of other locations in terms of stocking decisions. However, the multi-echelon assumption is a better reflection of reality as the stocking positions of related locations in a supply network do influence each other.

A Multi-Echelon Network Explained

One of the greatest impediments to understanding the concept of multi-echelon software functionality is confusing it with the frequently used term "multi-echelon supply chains." As we just discussed, an echelon is simply a layer of locations within a supply network. Any supply network with more than one echelon is considered multi-echelon. However, when an MRP and DRP system plan a multi-echelon supply network, does that make the software multi-echelon? Multi-echelon software refers to a specific technology while the other term—multi-echelon supply chains—refers simply to the physical setup of a supply chain. Separating these terms is not made any easier due to the fact that a number of vendors have attempted to blur this distinction in order to obscure the fact that they lack multi-echelon functionality. While all supply planning applications deal with multi-echelon networks, not all supply planning applications have the ability to plan the supply network using the mathematics of multi-echelon inventory optimization. This distinction is simple, yet vital to understanding multi-echelon software functionality and to making good software selection decisions.

Example of a Multi-Echelon Network

A multi-echelon supply network is simply a network of locations, which has multiple levels, or echelons. The simplest multi-echelon supply network is made up of two echelons. The easiest way to understand this relationship is to see it represented graphically. Both a single-echelon network and a multi-echelon network are illustrated on the next page.

Multi-Echelon Planning Explained

Single Echelon Supply Network

Suppliers

DCs

Customers

Multi Echelon Supply Network

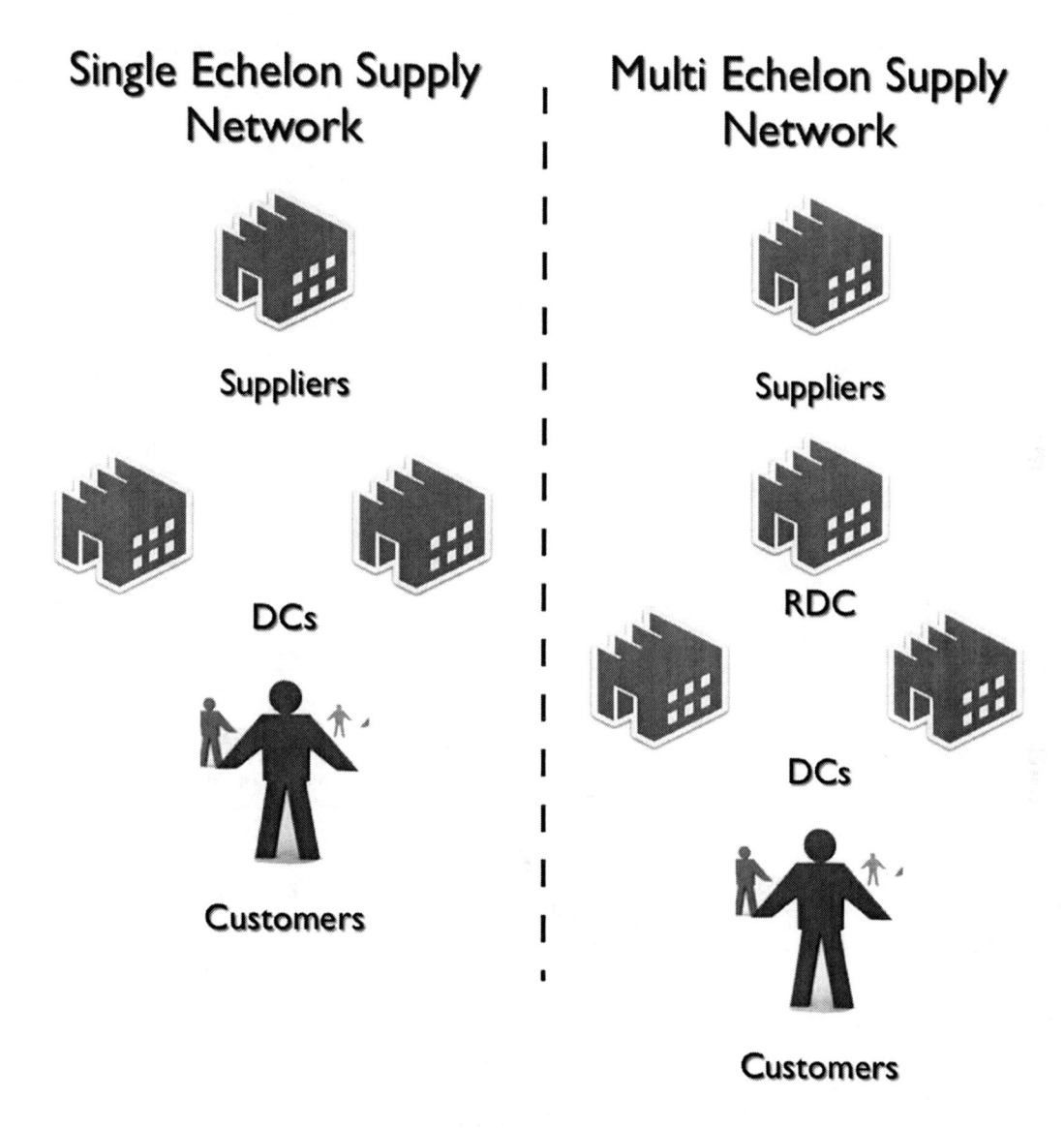

Suppliers

RDC

DCs

Customers

As the company on the left side only controls the stocking location and quantity for the DCs (distribution centers), and in this example the DCs do not supply each other, the supply network is a single echelon. However, only small companies have a supply network that resembles this configuration. Most companies of any size have a regional distribution center. If the company on the left were to begin to allow inter-DC transfers, they would *also have a multi-echelon network. In fact, a single-echelon supply network can quickly become multi-echelon by the simple act of accepting material from a supplier in just one location (for instance, to benefit from a volume discount) rather than taking separate shipments from the supplier to multiple facilities.*

The Multi Echelon Problem of Aggregated Purchasing for Discounts

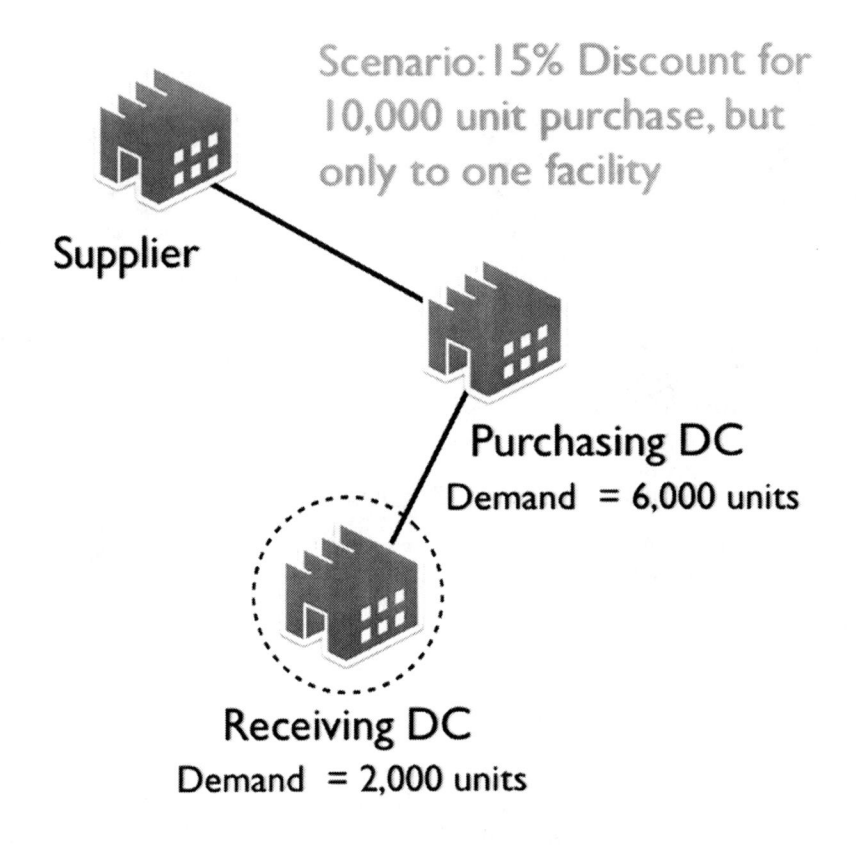

Scenario: 15% Discount for 10,000 unit purchase, but only to one facility

Supplier

Purchasing DC
Demand = 6,000 units

Receiving DC
Demand = 2,000 units

Circuitous / indirect product transfer to attain a 10,000 quantity discount purchase. However, the initial purchasing DC cannot consume all of the supply.

While most companies have multi-echelon networks, not all supply networks are of equal complexity from the perspective of multi-echelon. The more locations, and the more echelons (regional DCs, which feed DCs, which feed forward stocking locations, etc.), the more complex the multi-echelon problem becomes, and the more beneficial the implementation of MEIO software would be. Service parts networks are known for having a high number of echelons due partially to their need for forward stocking locations that can quickly service expensive equipment, thus minimizing equipment downtime. Service parts networks have the additional complexity of needing to move repairable items to locations in the supply network where they can be serviced. Therefore, it is not surprising that one of the early innovators in multi-echelon inventory optimization was MCA Solutions, a vendor that focused on the service parts market. Furthermore, the earliest papers on multi-echelon and inventory optimization were directed toward optimizing service parts networks, not finished goods networks.

MEIO's Value Adds to the Planning Process

Lack of understanding of how multi-echelon inventory optimization adds value to the planning process is an impediment to understanding the technology itself. For this I turn to Dr. Calvin Lee, an expert in multi-echelon, who has this to say on the topic of multi-echelon complexity:

> Managing inventory in a multi-echelon network versus in a single-echelon network presents major pitfalls. One is the failure to achieve true network inventory optimization because replenishment strategies are applied to one echelon without regard to its impact on the other echelons. A network view of inventory usage up and down the demand chain is absent when you are only dealing with a single echelon of locations. The complexities of managing inventory increase significantly for a multi-echelon distribution network with multiple tiers of locations (i.e., a network comprising a central warehouse and downstream customer-facing locations). All locations are under the internal control of a single enterprise.

One of the important points made by Dr. Lee is the very common failure to achieve true network inventory optimization, because replenishment strategies are applied to one echelon without regard to its impact on the other echelons. This is referred to as "independent" or "sequential location" planning and is described in the graphic below.

Traditional vs. Multi-Echelon Planning

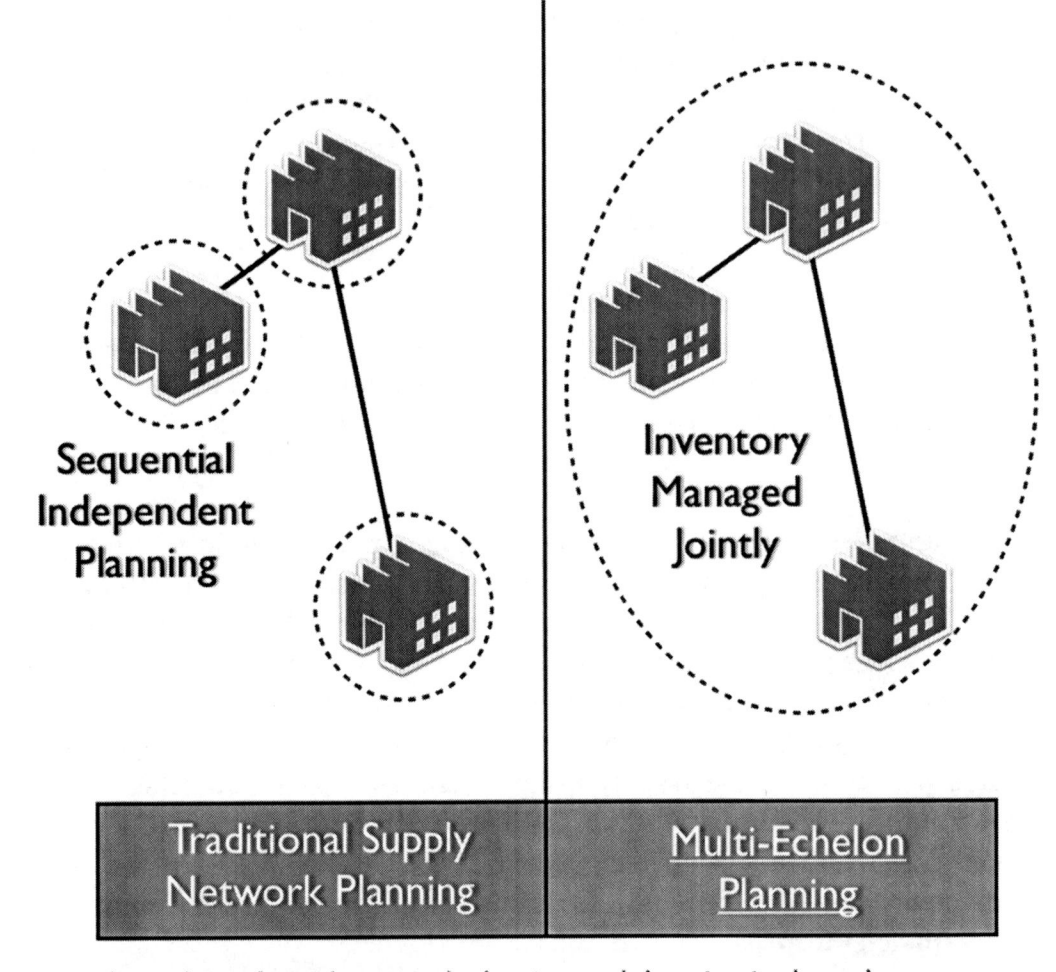

Sequential Independent Planning	Inventory Managed Jointly
Traditional Supply Network Planning	Multi-Echelon Planning

In traditional supply network planning, each location is planned independently of the other locations. Multi-echelon planning is more complex, and co-plans the locations as an inventory "pool."

Taking Dr. Lee's Multi-Echelon Test

Dr. Lee laid out the following criteria for whether a software application is actually MEIO in his well-known MEIO white paper, "Multi-Echelon Inventory Optimization," which I still consider the best white paper written on MEIO. I have paraphrased his bullets below (and changed some of the descriptions slightly). I have also provided my own commentary (which is parenthetically next to each bullet point). I do not agree with Dr. Lee on each point; however, in explaining what Dr. Lee laid out, and in some cases offering an opposing viewpoint, I hope to offer you a thorough understanding of each of the criteria to help you make up your own mind.

1. *Forecast Only at the DCs:* Avoid multiple independent forecast updates in each echelon by allowing the primary demand signal at the DCs to drive the forecasts in all echelons.

2. *Effective Lead-time:* Users must have the ability to compare the stocking position at different locations by calculating effective lead-times. (To find out more about this capability, see this post: http://www.scmfocus.com/inventoryoptimizationmultiechelon/2010/01/effective-lead-time-and-multi-echelon/.)

3. *Account for All Lead-time Variations:* (I would classify this as a "nice to have." Some vendors such as Servigistics and ToolsGroup can do this; however, software that cannot do this can still be multi-echelon and can still add significant value to the supply plan.)

4. *Monitor and Manage the Bullwhip Effect:* The Bullwhip Effect is the well-known problem of over-response due partially to the fact that locations are planned independently of one another (locations are planned independently between organizations as well and the Bullwhip Effect exists both inside and outside of one company's supply network). Dr. Lee lists this as a separate item from point two, but I would argue that point two takes care of this.

5. *Enable Visibility Up and Down the Supply Chain:* (All supply planning software should do this, but it is not distinctly a multi-echelon criterion. Visibility could be provided simply by a very good interface.)

6. *Synchronize Order Strategies:* "Synchronizing the order cycles at the DCs with RDC (regional distribution center) operations reduced lead-times and lead-time variations between RDC and DCs." (A multi-echelon approach makes this possible because the enterprise controls how and when a product enters and leaves the RDC. This is a nuanced criterion in that it is also rarely discussed. The concept of managing ordering such that it is coordinated between locations is a great leap conceptually for most supply chain practitioners.)

7. *Offer Differentiated Service Levels:* "The RDC can provide different service levels (for the same product) to different DCs. A multi-echelon approach makes this possible, because the enterprise controls how and when a product leaves the DC." (Here Dr. Lee is speaking of different service levels per location rather than different service levels per customer. Differentiated service levels per customer would fall into the category of inventory optimization.)

8. *Correctly Model the Interactive Effects of Alternative Replenishment Strategies of One Echelon or Another:* (I place this in the category of simulation and agree that multi-echelon software should have the ability to perform simulation effectively. Luckily, as is described in Chapter 7: "MEIO and Simulation," simulation tends to be a strength of MEIO software.)

Evaluating the Relative Importance of the Criteria

Different people will read this list of criteria and come to their own conclusions as to the most important features of multi-echelon planning, but I consider the second point to be the most important. While at one time the ability to plan locations at different service levels was state-of-the-art, some MEIO software have moved even beyond that to other approaches and to service level aggregation above the product location, enabling them to plan at the customer or contract (a contract is a special MEIO capability for service parts planning that supports a large piece of equipment such as an airplane or earth-moving construction equipment; the equipment is the "contract").

The criterion of not forecasting at internal supply network locations is very important. It dovetails with the concept of managing all the inventory-carrying locations as an "inventory pool" and is quite different from the present way of thinking about this topic. Forecasting only at forward locations also has the added benefit of reducing the forecast error. It is also the most accurate way of representing demand to MEIO software. Most supply chain organizations create forecasts, which are allocated to the initial point of demand. Distribution centers that sell to a customer have the sales orders allocated against the location that fulfills the customer demand. That part is simple; however the interesting question is whether the regional distribution centers (RDCs) should also have a forecast. The answer is that they do not need one as they derive their demand from the forecast at the DCs. In practice some companies still create RDC forecasts, but with multi-echelon software, it is unnecessary to create any forecast except the forecast at the DC. In fact, this is required in order to allow multi-echelon planning to perform all of its functions properly.

Understanding Effective Lead-Time

Effective lead-time is not an intuitive concept, as I can relay from my experience explaining the concept to a number of people. I was exposed to the concept of effective lead-time for the first time through MCA Solutions' manuals, and I certainly did not understand effective lead-time the first time I was exposed to it. Since then, I have written several articles at SCM Focus positioning effective lead-time as the foundational concept of multi-echelon planning. No other supply planning method (MRP/DRP, heuristic, allocation, or cost optimization) has this concept or capability and as such, none are as efficient at locating inventory as MEIO applications. Effective lead-time—the concept that stocking positions are determined and affected by connected locations and the ability to model this in the decision making—is why this functionality is more accurate in determining *where* inventory should be stocked than the other methods of supply planning.

Effective lead-time is a capability that any application calling itself MEIO should have, even if the vendor chooses to call it something different. Effective lead-time is only resident in multi-echelon systems.

- Effective lead-time is the total lead-time required to deliver the product to its final destination. It is variable and dependent on the stocking positions of higher echelons in the supply network. When higher-level locations must be called upon to satisfy a demand, lead-time is lengthened. Therefore, the effective lead-time is always conditional and ever-changing depending on the circumstance of the demand.

- Effective lead-time is not the standard static lead-time between two locations that is brought in through the master data (which is how most supply chain professionals are trained to understand lead-times), but instead it is a calculated value. Unlike standard lead-times, effective lead-times are situational. It is the lead-time required in the particular circumstance or scenario in question. With multi-echelon software, the lead-times between the DC and RDC change depending upon the stocking quantity and the service level at the RDC. Software that lacks multi-echelon capability keeps the same static lead time regardless of the inventory held at the RDC.

- Effective lead-time is best explained with the support of a graphic, which I have included on the next page. With it, notice how the effective lead-time is calculated and how it changes based on how many items are demanded.

Quantity Held at a Location and the **Effective Lead Time**

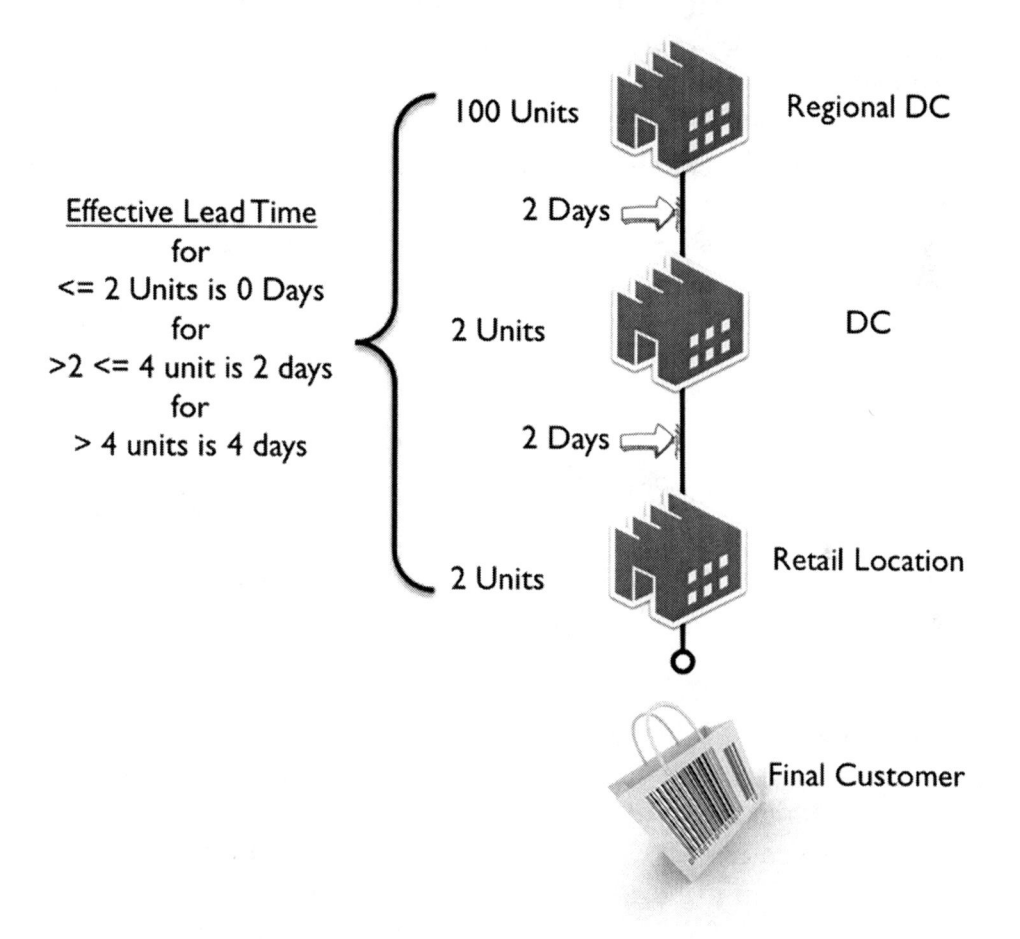

Effective Lead Time
for
<= 2 Units is 0 Days
for
>2 <= 4 unit is 2 days
for
> 4 units is 4 days

- 100 Units — Regional DC
- 2 Days
- 2 Units — DC
- 2 Days
- 2 Units — Retail Location
- Final Customer

In this example, the effective lead-time is the lead-time experienced by a customer at a retail location. Note the chain effect: their effective lead-time increases as the quantity demanded increases as more demand stocks out locations higher in the supply network. The numbers here are kept small in order to improve the clarity of the explanation.

A key assumption is that this is a single product supply chain. All locations carry only one product. The example above shows that while the actual lead-time stays the same between the locations, depending upon the demand versus what is stocked at the various locations, the effective lead-time changes depending upon how high in the multi-echelon supply chain it is necessary to go to obtain inventory.

If lead-time is not adjusted as circumstances change, the RDC and DC are not actually pooling inventory or auto-adjusting for each others' inventory positions. Without effective lead-time, the natural inclination is to position inventory "closer to the customer" at the DC. Often the result of this is too much inventory positioned forward in the supply network, which at some point will require more costly inter-echelon stock transfers in order to meet demand. (Stock transfers between forward locations are less efficient than stock transfers from higher rearward locations to forward locations.) This is the exact problem that exists in many service supply chains— automotive service parts supply chains are a perfect example.

Focus On Automotive Service Supply Chains

The Problems in Automotive Service Supply Chains
The automotive service sector has some of the least-efficient supply chains found in industry. One major reason for this is that the OEMs (Ford, Honda, etc.) are not in control of the entire supply chain. They must contend with a hodgepodge of "retailers" (dealers) that are diffused and not connected by ownership structure. When consultants for software vendors that specialize in MEIO service parts planning use their software to analyze an account, they often find that parts are simply too far forward in the supply network. This is because auto service parts networks are generally not well integrated. Fill rates are managed locally and local managers attempt to move parts to where they will eventually be consumed, rather than keep them in the regional distribution center where they can be accessed by multiple locations. This causes a "tragedy of the commons," with each dealer attempting to maximize their service level without consideration

for the overall supply network. In this situation, MEIO service parts planning software will typically move more expensive and slower turning parts out of the dealers and back up to the next echelon in the network (typically controlled by the OEM). Generally, the independent-dealer model continues to work against rational inventory pooling and effective supply network inventory management.

A Better Design

A much more effective arrangement than having every dealer attempt to manage its inventory is for the dealers to pool their parts at a local depot and for the depot to manage the parts for them. Daily local "milk runs" would ensure parts flow to the dealers and would reduce the inventory turnover of parts at the dealer location. The network of these depots or regional distribution centers (RDCs) can then be made large enough to be electronically connected and to have their inventory represented in a Web order fulfillment system. Such a system can better match supply and demand than can a series of disconnected dealers all trying to manage smaller amounts of inventory locally, and it can do so at a lower cost. In fact, in some cases this happens. I do not mean to imply that all OEM networks are managed identically, but by in large, the industry is missing an obvious opportunity to improve the parts management.

The lesson of multi-echelon supply planning is that no location-specific inventory management system can match the efficient inventory placement of MEIO software. Multi-echelon systems can look at the entire network and can plan the entire network as if it is a single inventory location (with the mathematics to support effective lead-times).

The automotive dealer system is one example of an industry where the inventory is poorly planned due to its particular retail ownership structure and incentives. I researched the accessibility of parts online and found that dealers are considerably behind the times in online retailing as well. There simply seems to be little that automotive parts distribution does well, and the cost to serve customers is exceedingly high. Because of this general disinterest in improvement, automotive parts networks will likely be one of the last sectors to install MEIO software. Auto dealers have in the past simply passed their inefficiency on in the form of higher parts costs to consumers.

Interestingly, even though the automotive sector is a high-profile industry, most analysts will cover a company's new products without addressing service capability as a brand differentiator. *Consumer Reports* has been one of the few publications to measure product quality and they maintain a very well-known focus on automotive quality. It is an influential publication that some people use to help them make car purchases. However, while the publication covers repair frequency as a function of design, manufacturing and use, they do not cover repair costs, which are partially a function of the service part supply chain (both in terms of part availability and part cost).

Where Is the Service Level Being Set?
There are several ways to perform multi-echelon planning, and not every vendor performs multi-echelon planning in the same way. It is critical to match how the vendor sets service levels with the company's service level requirements. In my experience, which is also mirrored by others, this can be complicated when companies do not spend enough time figuring out how they want to manage service levels. Determination of service levels and where to set them is tricky as well as political because it gets to the heart of how the company manages its customer relationships. In Chapter 3: "Inventory Optimization Explained," I discussed briefly that service levels are more understandable and logical to businesses than the costs used in cost optimization. That, of course, is the first hurdle. The second hurdle is getting consensus on what the service level settings should be.

It is very easy to spend a great deal of time discussing this topic without coming to a conclusion. However, companies can begin making headway on the application's settings before they buy the MEIO application. When companies are considering MEIO software, I recommend that internal discussions begin as soon as possible on setting service levels. These discussions and any resulting decisions should be documented, and the documentation—which outlines what the future service level design will be—should be shared with all interested parties. The document is a living document that is repeatedly updated with the changes required to attain consensus. The intent of this documentation is to bring disagreements

Multi-Echelon Planning Explained

to the surface and to do so earlier rather than later in the implementation process. The later in the process disagreements develop, the more expensive it is to make changes to the design. Having a tool helps make the decision on where to set service levels as one can rapidly understand the impact and cost of different service level settings.

MEIO offers capabilities that the implementing company did not have access to previously. Companies that intend to select and implement MEIO software should have the necessary internal discussions as to how and where they want to control their supply planning with service levels. The way the implementing company is current performing supply planning will if unaltered, will not be able to fully leverage MEIO's capabilities. The decision of where to set service levels should be known prior to any MEIO software selection. Of course this means understanding the options for service levels. To this end I have listed the options below.

In MEIO software, service levels can be set by the following:

- At the location
- At the product-location combination
- At the group location
- At the customer
- At a product mix
- *At the contract/equipment

*Setting the service level "at the contract/equipment" can be a customer service contract or an actual piece of equipment. This functionality is specifically for the service parts market. Therefore, while managing service levels by contract can be found in service parts planning software that uses MEIO technology, it is not found in MEIO vendors for non-service parts planning. "At the location" sets an overall service level for the location in the supply network.

Each option comes with its own list of pros and cons, which I detail on the following pages.

Setting Service Levels at the Location

Pros
- Easy to understand
- Fits with how some companies currently manage their service levels

Cons
- Does not apply directly to the service level at the customer
- Relatively inflexible way of setting service levels
- Does not leverage the full capability of true MEIO solutions

Setting Service Levels at the Product-Location Combination

The number of areas in the application where the service level must be maintained is greatly multiplied when using the product-location combination. However, conceptually, it is very similar to maintaining service levels at the location.

Pros
- Easy to understand
- Fits with how some companies currently manage their service levels

Cons
- Does not apply directly to the service level at the customer
- Relatively inflexible way of setting service levels
- Does not leverage the full capability of MEIO solutions
- Even more effort to manage than "at the location," because it results in more places for service levels to be changed

Setting Service Levels at the Group Location

Really just an adjustment to setting service levels at the location. Instead locations are aggregated. Has all the same advantages and disadvantages as setting service levels at the location.

Pros
- Easy to understand
- Fits with how some companies currently manage their service levels

Cons
- Does not apply directly to the service level at the customer
- Relatively inflexible way of setting service levels
- Does not leverage the full capability of true MEIO solutions

Where to Set Service Level?

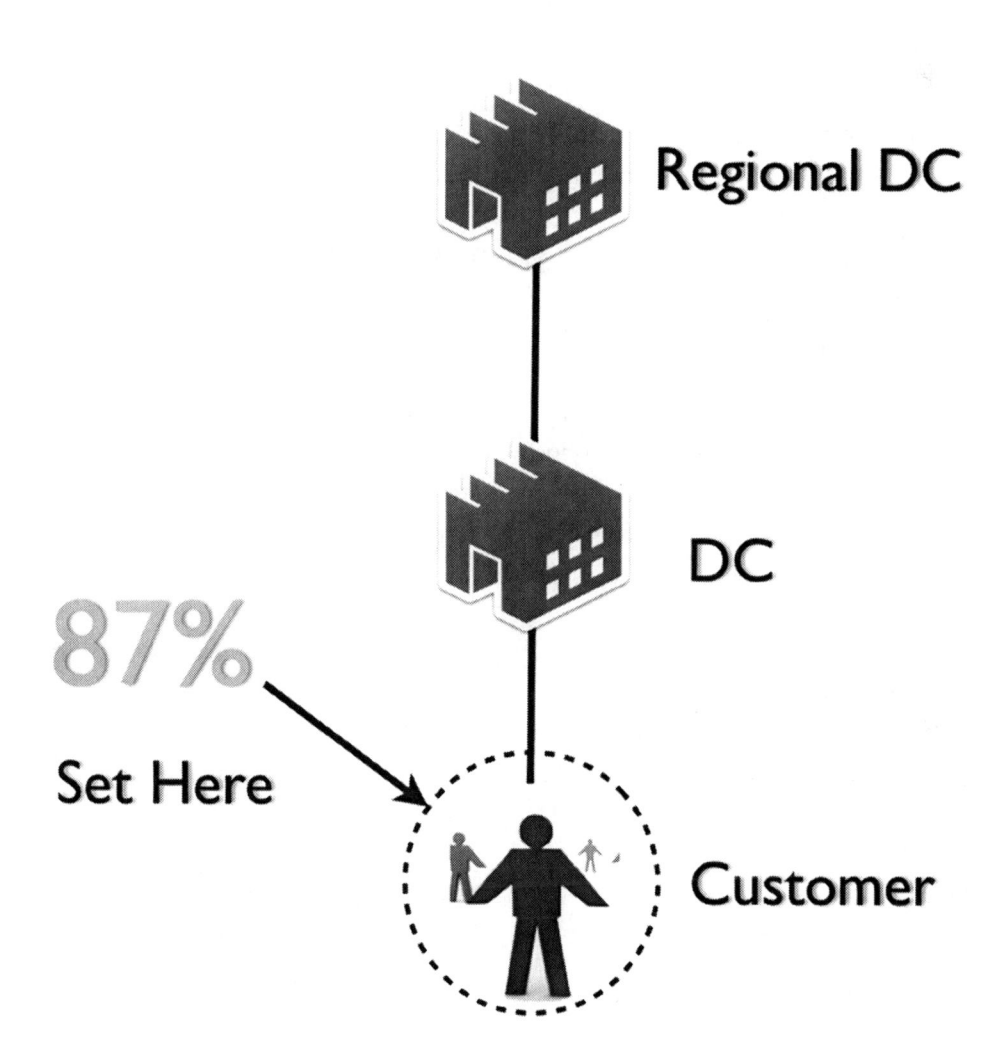

87% Set Here → Customer

Regional DC → DC → Customer

Setting Service Levels at the Customer

Taken from the service management market, the concept of managing the supply network by assigning different service levels per customer has become a topic of interest in the finished goods market. This is fully explained in Chapter 8: "MEIO and Service Level Agreements."

Pros

- Provides the ability to charge different prices for different levels of service
- Reduces the maintenance required for changing and updating service levels
- Allows the output to be used by both supply planning and sales

Cons

- Not appropriate for companies that do not differentiate service levels by customer nor engage their customers in service level agreements
- Tends to create politically challenging and protracted disagreement on the various service levels (i.e., the priority) of different customers or lines of business

Setting Service Levels at a Product Mix

Some companies such as those in consumer packaged goods are responsible for hitting service targets on a mix of products that are provided to a variety of customers. The company can then offer differing service levels per product or per time of year, as long as they attain the overall service level number.

Pros

- Can lead to a shared understanding of the trade-offs between service levels and inventory that must be used depending upon the product mix
- Is not always, but can be, easier for the business to decide on the service levels per product mix than per customer

Cons

- More difficult to administer than simply setting service levels by the customer

Setting Service Levels at the Contract

Used only in the service parts market, this setting allows a specific, usually quite expensive, piece of equipment such as an airplane or a piece of heavy construction equipment to have a specific uptime or availability. Service parts planning software can switch from the service level metric to the availability metric in order to support contracts. Availability is how often the equipment is available for use, or colloquially its "uptime."

Pros

- Provides very powerful functionality that plans all the parts necessary to support the uptime of equipment
- Estimates the cost of supporting a particular piece of equipment, which supports a specific costing of the contract for that equipment

Cons

- Does not apply for companies that do not work in the service parts market

The Mistaken Assumption about Service Levels at the Location

Discussing where service levels are managed brings us to a common and unexamined assumption among the majority of supply chain professionals. This assumption, which was touched on in several of the bullet points above, is that service levels set at locations or at product groups will result in a specific service level provided to a customer—that the allocation would result in inventory provided to the right customer by roughly approximating the agreed-upon service level promised to the client. Interestingly, there is no evidence to support this assumption, nor is it an accurate assumption given the present level of software capability within most supply chain organizations. This leads to the following important question.

Considering Who Is the Ultimate Consumer of Service Level

This first assumption then connects to a second, unexamined assumption about service level management—that is, that the supply chain itself is the consumer of the service level. Some very experienced supply chain professionals may initially disagree that this assumption is held. After all, it is never, in fact, explicitly stated. However, if you analyze how most supply chain companies manage service levels, this assumption is clearly implied. Companies will often assign very specific metrics to all the locations in the supply network and then manage them, because companies without MEIO (which is the vast majority of companies) *lack the ability to directly tie their stocking levels to the customer service level.* Therefore, they default to what they can control, which is the service levels at the individual locations of the supply network. However, the customer, not the supply chain, is the consumer of the service levels produced by supply chain planning and execution. All service levels, be they measured and set at the product location, at the line item, or any other area, are ultimately surrogates for the only service level that has meaning—the service level to the customer. This is related to Dr. Lee's point as to what makes software multi-echelon: a forecast that is entered at the DC, where demand is sent to the customer.

This is not to say that the service level to the customer is unrelated to the service levels at different locations, since they obviously are. However, they are not the same thing. As described in Chapter 3: "Inventory Optimization Explained," the higher in the service level hierarchy the service level is set, the more degrees of freedom or flexibility the system is being given, and the more the system is effectively determining the optimal quantity of inventory between product locations. As the section on effective lead-time explained, multi-echelon functionality is the ability to treat the entire supply network as if it were one stocking location—one location, but with a complex combination of constantly changing effective lead-times based on continually altering demand circumstances. The optimal end state is to set service levels in a way that is consistent with business objectives and then to have software that allows planners to "close their eyes" and have the system decide the appropriate service level per customer-product location. The graphic on the next page describes the desirable end state for a company that wants to perform supply planning in a way that matches differentiated service levels.

Service Level Setting at the Customer

Service Levels at the Product Location Adjust

Customer: SLA #1 — 97%
Customer: SLA #2 — 85%

MEIO Software

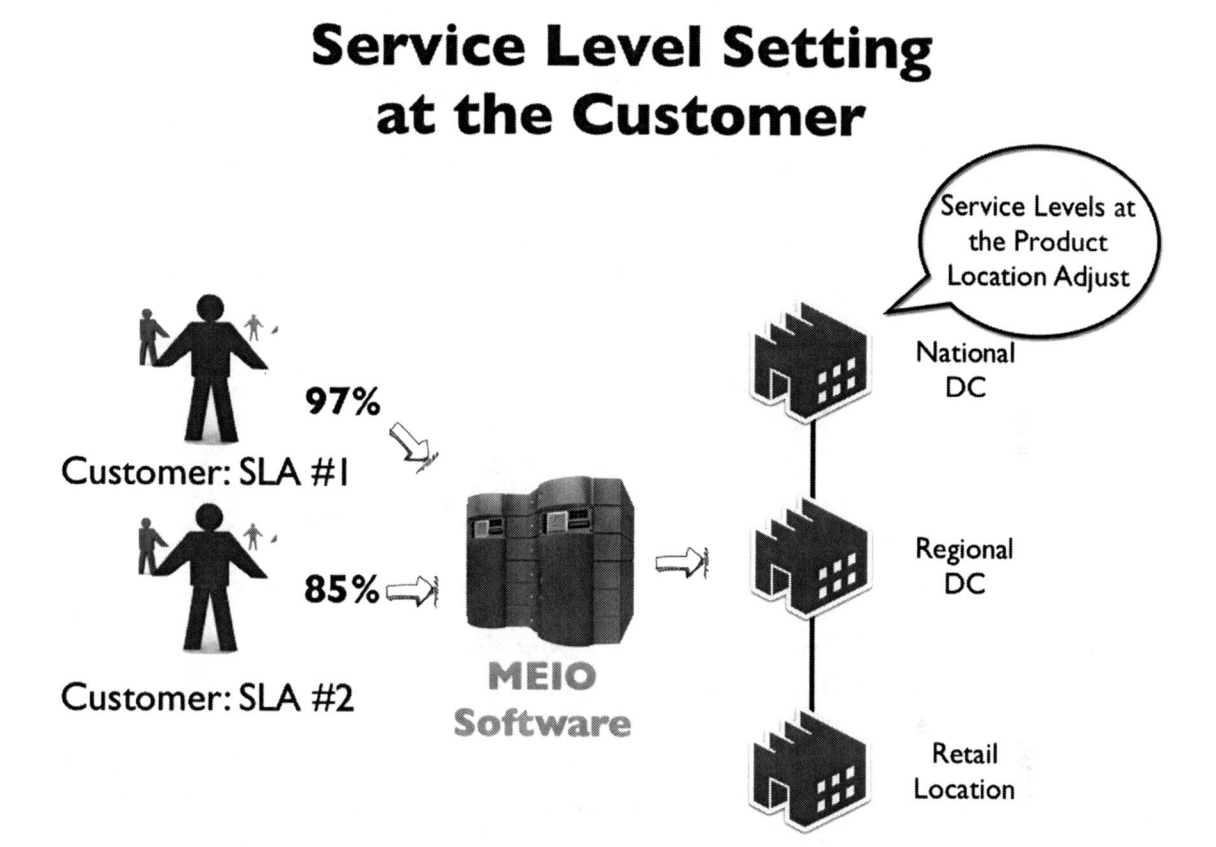

National DC
Regional DC
Retail Location

Making Service Level Changes

Following is a screen from Logility that shows how the inventory targets are reviewed and changed in a very direct manner. With MEIO software, this is the most important process step performed by the planners.

		Total Demand ($/Month)	Total Demand (Units/Month)	On-Hand Inventory Investment ($)	On-Hand Inventory (Units)
Proposed		$645,787	32,498	$238,497	10,359
In-Production		$703,117	33,472	$400,156	13,979
Difference		($57,330)	-974	($161,659)	-3,621

Total SKUs: 6   Total Locations: 5   Total Items: 10

Filtered data is up to date. Forward Horizon: 24 Months

Item Navigation

Item	Select	Location	SKU	SKU Description	Accept/Reject	Safety Stock (Days)	Exception Count	Average Demand (Units/Month)	Demand Uncertainty (%/Month)	Service Level (%)	Lead Time (Days)	On-Hand Inventory (Days)	On-Hand Inventory Investment ($)
Details	☐	RDC1	SP24	FG Product 24		8.7	1	30,485	36%		1	8.7	$165,674
Details	☐	NDC	SP21	FG Product 21		48.4	1	909	95%		2	51.5	$70,054
Details	☐	V2	RM2	Raw Material Type 2		11.8	4	774	47%		9	11.8	$2,081
Details	☐	RDC3	SP25	FG Product 25		7.8	1	31	40%	95.0%	1	7.8	$174
Details	☐	RDC2	SP25	FG Product 25		7.4	1	31	40%		1	7.4	$167
Details	☐	NDC	RM2	Raw Material Type 2		1.8	1	225	50%		0	1.8	$93
Details	☐	NDC	SP29	FG Product 29		7.7	1	13	43%		2	10.8	$83
Details	☐	RDC1	SP29	FG Product 29		7.4	1	13	43%	95.0%	1	7.4	$81
Details	☐	RDC3	SP28	FG Product 28		7.8	2	11	46%	95.0%	1	7.8	$52
Details	☐	NDC	SP28	FG Product 28		10.4	1	6	60%		2	13.9	$37

Here different items show the effect of additions of safety stock. Notice the information density, yet the clarity of the screen. The view offers an intuitive understanding of what is happening to changes in the planning state of these products.

The Issue of a Strong Versus a Weak Linkage Between Service Levels and Inventory Levels

The less direct the linkage between service levels and inventory levels, the weaker the control over the supply network. The weaker the control, the more the inventory and the supply planning parameters must be tinkered with. Much of this tinkering is referred to as "planning" or "adjusting the plan." Companies that spend the time to track these changes often find that a high percentage of products are being manually changed on an ongoing basis. These changes are often made first by using offline analysis in Excel, which then brings up the topic of what is really controlling planning: the expensive planning system, which was thought to greatly improve the company's ability to plan, or Excel? The source of these changes is not only planners, but also directors and even vice presidents. One company I am familiar with still manages inventory by days' supply target, a pre-MEIO and actually pre-heuristic method of managing inventory levels.

Target Days of Supply

Being able to control the target stocking level by a service level is unique to MEIO. Some may disagree with this statement and point to the target days of supply, which is a way of maintaining a desired overall stock level. However, if one looks into how the target days' supply is derived in such commonly-used supply planning applications as SAP APO SNP, the target days' supply simply leverages the lot size functionality by increasing or decreasing the lot size based upon the forecast. That is, rather than hard-coding the lot size, the target days' supply functionality *adjusts the lot size as needed*. If the SNP optimizer is used, the adherence to the target days' supply is enforced with the safety stock penalty cost. More on this topic is available at the post below:

http://www.scmfocus.com/sapplanning/2011/11/05/how-soft-constraints-work-with-soft-constraints-days-supply-and-safety-stock-penalty-costs/

The formula for days' supply is the following:

Days' Supply = Total Inventory / Average Daily Consumption

Certainly, maintaining an adjustable stock level is desirable, and as any supply planner knows, one of the most valuable barometers of whether the stock is in the correct range is how the target days' supply compares to the planned days' supply.

However, important questions to ask are, "what is the correct target days' supply," and "how does the target days' supply relate to the desired service level?" The answer to the first question is that companies generally set the target days' supply based upon experience. However as is described in several paragraphs, this target can be based on averages for large groups of products and may not always be particularly accurate. The answer to the second question is that while a high days' supply relates to a higher service level and a low days' supply to a lower service level, generally, the target days' supply *does not correlate to any specific service level*. Therefore, while the target days' supply is a rough measure of whether the planned stocking level is within a range, it is not a mechanism for setting stock levels based upon service levels.

Secondly, there are some issues that should be addressed in using a days' supply with an optimizer. Essentially, simply maintaining a days' supply limits what mathematicians would call the number of degrees of freedom of the optimizer, or in laymen's terms, the number of free variables and the flexibility that is provided to the optimizer. In this way, days' supply becomes a training wheel for the optimizer, which is important because an optimizer is not set up to derive a good solution based upon costs. Days' supply is a pre-MRP method of performing supply planning. In fact, days' supply, set at every location in the supply network, could be its own supply planning method. The rule could simply be to attempt to meet demand while maintaining the preset days' supply.

As companies begin to implement MEIO, these older approaches to supply planning as well as the degree to which manual adjustment is necessary, will need to be addressed. It makes little sense to implement a highly flexible, self-adjusting system if the mindset within the supply chain organization is still calibrated to performing supply planning in a pre-MEIO state. Many people comfortable with simpler approaches may never understand or appreciate MEIO, and that is perfectly natural. However, when a set of processes is designed around one level of technology, the processes should not stay the same when a more advanced form is introduced.

Supply Chain Precision as a Discussion Point

As important as the topic is, it's very rare for supply chain professionals to discuss the precision of the controls within any supply planning system. The limitations of the system are simply accepted without much questioning, even though the precision of control over the supply plan dictates the necessary amount of intervention into the system, which of course relates strongly to the business effort and maintenance required to work with the application. Here, change management becomes important because things should be done differently with MEIO. However, "change management" requires true education of people and true knowledge management systems to support and reinforce this education.

Conclusion

Much less emphasis is placed on multi-echelon planning functionality than inventory optimization functionality even though both work in conjunction in MEIO software. It is not accurate to consider one to be more important that the other. Many people think that multi-echelon planning describes the act of planning a multi-leveled supply network when in fact it is a distinct mathematical functionality that only MEIO applications have. Multi-echelon planning is not easy for even experienced supply chain professionals to understand, and a major reason for this is that it works fundamentally differently from MRP/DRP and APS systems. These systems, which assume static (transportation mode independent) lead-times, are currently the most widely installed and their assumptions are quite naturally the accepted ones for those who work in the field. With the term "multi-echelon," my observation is that we have yet to get past the buzzword phase into a real understanding of what multi-echelon means, at least for the majority of supply chain professionals exposed to the concept. Furthermore, the promotional activities of several vendors have commingled multi-echelon planning with the physical multi-echelon supply network, when in fact the two terms describe two different things and, as a result, have set back attempts to educate people as to the proper meaning of the term.

Multi-echelon planning software provides a great opportunity for service supply chains that need to ensure they keep expensive and less frequently repaired items at the RDC. However, all but the simplest supply chains benefit from multi-echelon functionality. Effective lead-times are the central concept in multi-echelon planning. While lead-times for the same mode between locations do not change in the short-term (in the long-term, the supply network can be reconfigured), *effective* lead-times are changing continuously depending on the circumstance of the demand and the stocking positions of the related locations. The effective lead-times must continually change in the application's calculations in order for software to be functional for multi-echelon planning. This, combined with inventory optimization functionality, is what allows the software to properly position inventory in the right location and in the right quantity based on demand, current stocking position, and service levels.

It is important that everyone involved in a MEIO implementation or trained in MEIO software understands effective lead-time and its implications for planning. I have seen cases where the implementing company did not do nearly enough to explain MEIO and the planners interpreted the implemented system as carrying insufficient levels of inventory. The directors at this company asked the planners to keep their old pre-MEIO days' supply targets unchanged. Therefore, the effect of the MEIO implementation at this company was minimal. What was not understood is that MEIO will calculate a lower stocking level because MEIO systems can see the interactions between the locations in a way that non-MEIO systems cannot. If planners are using an older concept based upon less sophisticated mathematics as a reference point for how inventory should be calculated, they are less likely to accept the results of the MEIO system and will tend to override it, thus undermining the benefits of the system. If this happens, not only should the planners be blamed (which is a common area to be called out), but also the implementation, which did not accomplish its objective to educate both the planners and the supply chain planning decision makers. If a superior technology is given to people and they are properly educated as to how it works, and if it improves their condition, they will naturally gravitate toward using it. However, if they don't understand it, and don't know why the results it generates are different from what they are used to, they have every reason to reject it.

For those who are being exposed to this topic for the first time, it may take several readings and several weeks to understand all the implications of multi-echelon, because multi-echelon mathematics break with the previous assumptions held by most supply chain professionals. But "getting" something the first time should not necessarily be a goal of understanding complex subject matter. Complex subjects often require multiple exposures. Once understood, the multi-echelon method of inventory positioning in the supply network cannot help but be seen as significantly superior to the old ways of determining the best place for stock to be positioned. Although often ignored or trivialized, multi-echelon planning is truly an equal partner to inventory optimization in MEIO.

CHAPTER 5

How Inventory Optimization and Multi-Echelon Work Together to Optimize the Supply Plan

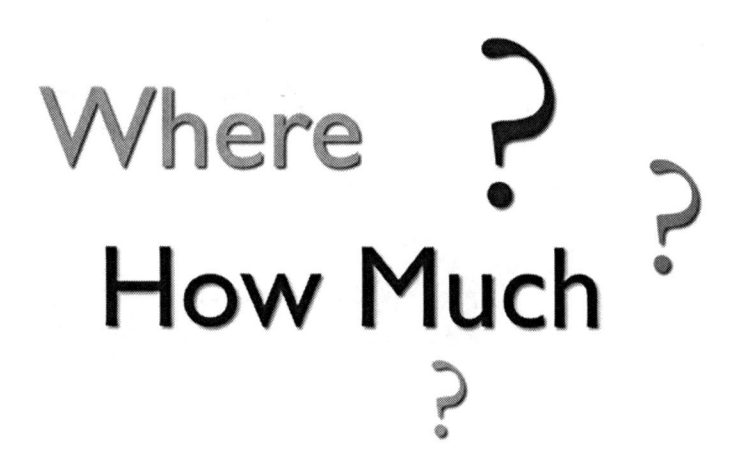

Where?

How Much?

What Questions are Being Answered with MEIO?
Now that we have covered inventory optimization and multi-echelon planning separately, we can discuss how they work together. Multi-echelon planning and inventory optimization answer two different questions, which are the most important questions in supply planning:

- Inventory Optimization: How much of a SKU should be stocked?
- Multi-Echelon: Where should the SKU be stocked?

How MEIO Actually Works

In order to demonstrate how this works, I have created the following graphic that represents a simple network with a limited number of options for where to allocate an extra fifty dollars in inventory investment. Once you understand this small model, you will understand the concept of MEIO and you can apply its concept to any number of product-location combinations; while larger models increase in complexity, the basic function is the same.

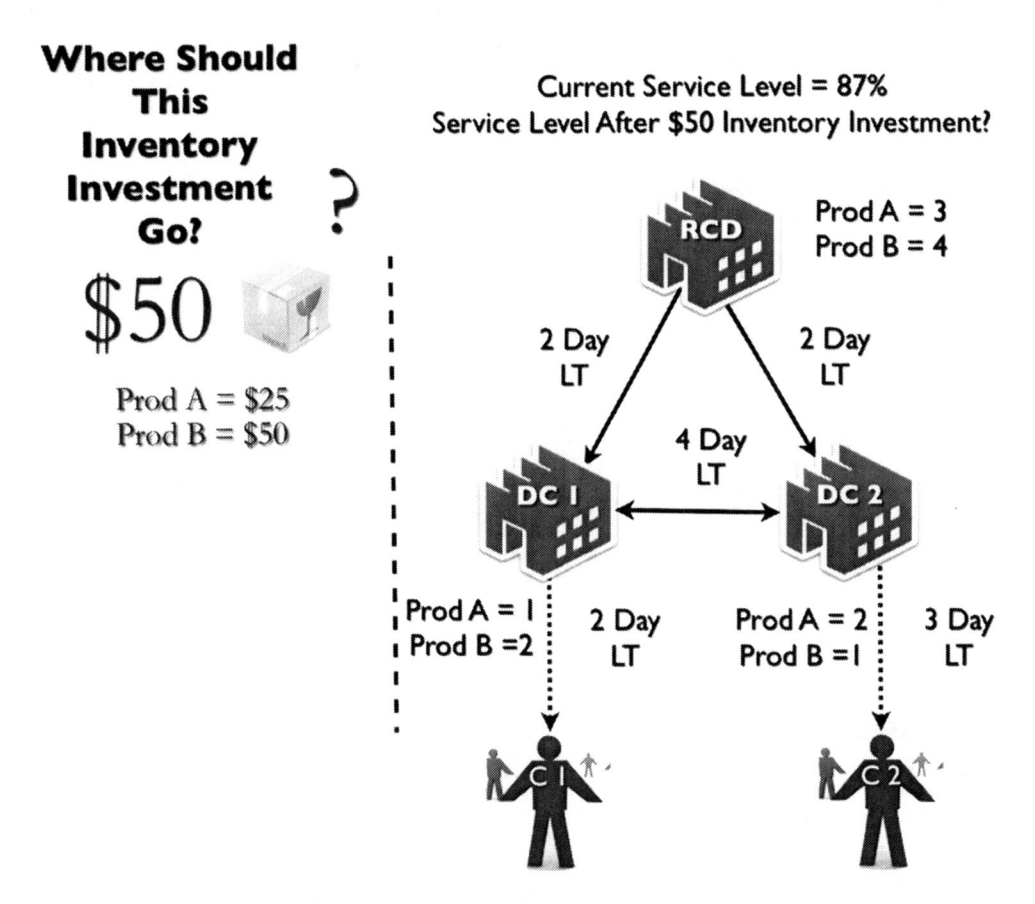

Where Should This Inventory Investment Go?

$50

Prod A = $25
Prod B = $50

Current Service Level = 87%
Service Level After $50 Inventory Investment?

RCD
Prod A = 3
Prod B = 4

2 Day LT → DC 1
2 Day LT → DC 2
DC 1 ↔ DC 2: 4 Day LT

DC 1: Prod A = 1, Prod B = 2 — 2 Day LT → C 1
DC 2: Prod A = 2, Prod B = 1 — 3 Day LT → C 2

From the above graphic we can observe a series of decisions. Each has inventory and service implications.

Supply Network Observations

The fifty dollars available to spend can either purchase two SKUs of Product A or one SKU of Product B.

The current network inventory is composed of thirteen units at a cost of $500, with Product A consuming $150 of inventory cost with six units and Product B consuming $350 with seven units.

Given the forecast history, the current planned stocking level, and the location, the current projected service level is eighty-seven percent.

There are nine different option combinations for which SKU to add inventory to and where to locate this new inventory. Therefore, the MEIO application would need to evaluate all of the following scenarios:

> 2 SKUs of A at the RDC (increases service level to 87.5 percent)
> 2 SKUs of A at DC1 (increases service level to 87.1 percent)
> 2 SKUs of A at DC2 (increases service level to 87.3 percent)
> 1 SKU of A at the RDC and 1 SKU of A at DC1 (increases service level to 87.2 percent)
> 1 SKU of A at the RDC and 1 SKU of A at DC2 (increases service level to 87.4 percent)
> 1 SKU of A at DC1 and 1 SKU of A at DC2 (increases service level to 87.7 percent)
> 1 SKU of B at RDC (increases service level to 87.2 percent)
> 1 SKU of B at DC1 (increases service level to 87.1 percent)
> 1 SKU of B at DC2 (increases service level to 87.3 percent)

Effective Lead-Time Observations

1. The effective lead-time for going from the RDC to Customer Two is five days (the time if DC2 stocks out of either SKU), while from the RDC to Customer One the effective lead-time is four days. This means that DC2 must be stocked slightly higher given the same average demand at Customer One and Customer Two.

2. The four-day lead-time for a stock transfer between DC1 and DC2 means that this would only occur in a situation where there is no stock at the RDC. Therefore, the MEIO model will have a tendency to hold stock back at the RDC if it is unclear whether the stock will be immediately required at either DC1 or DC2. Of course, it very much depends on the specific probabilities of a demand at DC1 versus DC2.

Understanding the Sample Model

To arrive at an optimal solution, the MEIO application would use a combination of the expected demand for a number of future periods at each location, the projected contribution to service levels, as well as the effective lead-times. The MEIO model would select Option Six as this option increases service levels the most (87.7 percent). If the model were given another fifty dollars in inventory investment, it would then recalculate the values for each option. In this case, since a recalculation of Option Six would lead to a low contribution to service levels (it now has more planned stock, which was added in the previous run), it would choose Option One, as it has the next highest increase in service levels (87.5 percent). Notice in this example that I am driving the model by increasing its inventory investment cap. However, I could also simply set a service level target (say, 88.5 percent for the entire supply network) and the system would continue to add inventory until it hit that target. After each iteration and selection of the highest-yielding option, the MEIO application must decide how specifically to increase stock using one of the following methods:

- A planned purchase order
- A planned stock transfer request
- In the case of service parts planning, a planned repair order

All of these are planned orders. These planned orders are then sent over to the execution system, which may or may not execute on these recommendations.

Differing Calculation Details

The above procedure has been over-simplified for educational purposes. Each vendor will differ on many details, including how this procedure is accomplished and how the list of potential stocking decisions is sorted at each iteration. These details and how vendors handle them should be understood during software selection in order to ensure that the company is using them as criteria to differentiate between vendors.

Aspects of the Sample Model Reflected in the Eventual Stocking Positions

If the lead-times to the customer from any location were all the same, then multi-echelon functionality would not be necessary. However, the lead-times are of course different. "Effective lead-time" is explained in Chapter 4: "Multi-Echelon Planning Explained." If you have any confusion on the topic, consider reviewing that chapter as it's important to understand effective lead-time completely to follow along with what comes next.

Redeployment

The transaction recommendations described in the model above are created during the normal planning run. They follow the normal supply chain flow of moving material from suppliers into the supply network and then moving material from parent or higher-echelon levels to child or lower-echelon levels. However, in some cases the ability to transfer stock (which is in lower echelons) from locations where it has a low likelihood of being consumed to locations where it has a higher likelihood of being consumed is an important capability. This is called redeployment, but also goes by the name of "inventory balancing" or "inventory rebalancing." Although redeployment is a greatly under-used function, it is an area of supply planning with high potential and MEIO applications are the best at doing it for reasons that I will discuss.

In terms of how MEIO applications generally perform redeployment, it comes down to the following:

- Service levels that drive deployed stock from low-opportunity locations to higher-opportunity locations
- The removal of the standard deployment restrictions that set a specific deployment path
- Costs of storage and transportation, which restrict the movement of product to those higher-opportunity locations to which it is more economical to

transfer the product. This makes very expensive cross-country movements the last option, and means that the closest locations have the advantage in receiving a transfer.

How various MEIO applications perform redeployment is more difficult to describe because of the different approaches taken by the different vendors. Some emphasize redeployment in their product, while others do not. MEIO vendors who also specialize in service parts planning tend to offer the strongest redeployment functionality. For instance, service parts planning vendor Servigistics has the ability to perform a separate yet comprehensive redeployment run where only redeployment stock transfer requests are created. This mode diverges from running the model with the normal location-to-location combinations that are set up during a deployment and allows any location to satisfy any other location. However, most non-service parts MEIO vendors choose a lighter form of redeployment. MEIO vendors that do not focus on the service parts market have redeployment functionality that is ordinarily integrated into the normal supply network run, and is typically more focused on redeployment at the lower-echelons in the supply network. For instance, Manhattan Associates works the following way with respect to redeployment:

> "We do have features in our MEIO like overstock transfer that can (based on configuration) automatically rebalance inventory, usually at the lower-echelon locations."
>
> — Rod Daugherty, Manhattan Associates

For more on redeployment, see this post:

http://www.scmfocus.com/inventoryoptimizationmultiechelon/2011/10/redeployment/

Planned Procurement or Production Orders?

Planned purchase orders may be converted in the ERP system to production orders for produced items. A recommendation to create a purchase order is simply a signal to the ERP system to introduce new inventory into the supply network.

MEIO applications do not focus on whether the introduced stock is procured or produced internally. As will be discussed later, while most MEIO vendors work this way at this step in the process, not all do. At least one vendor does not create transactions at all, but instead interoperates with the execution system on the basis of master data parameters.

Peeking Below the Hood of MEIO

Inventory optimization has one set of mathematics behind it, and multi-echelon planning has another. However, MEIO vendors combine them and have them perform their calculations iteratively. What is really quite amazing is that MEIO software does this for every product-location combination in the supply network and for every intermediate state between the starting inventory position until it hits either a service level or inventory investment cap (depending upon how the application is run). This stops the model from continuing to add inventory at a point declared within the application. A simplified version of the formula for the inventory optimization piece is shown below. Not all vendors use the same approach, but this graphic is a general approximation of how most of these applications work.

Basic Decision Making Criteria

$$\text{Maximize} \left(\frac{\text{Potential Contribution to Service Level}}{\text{Material Cost}} \right)$$

In the example above, there are only nine options to evaluate. However, as the number of factors to be compared increases (such as the product-location combinations and the number of SKUs), the number of overall options that the model must evaluate increases very rapidly, all of which can be predicted by combinatorial mathematics. Those who have calculated the total possible number combinations resulting from two dice being rolled have experience with exactly this type of analysis. MEIO models often have millions of options to compare in order to complete a single planning run. The model must develop a rating for every possible location combination, which it can then sort or rank, and based on this it selects the inventory transactions that will best contribute to service levels.

Transaction Recommendation Generating Applications vs. Master Data Update MEIO Applications
As mentioned earlier in this chapter, not all MEIO models create transactional recommendations (e.g., planned purchase orders, planned stock transfer orders, planned repair orders). SmartOps, for example, takes the approach of interacting with the ERP system through adjusting its inventory parameters. This is an approach that is appealing for companies looking for a simple integration with their ERP system and a quick implementation.

For MEIO applications that do create transaction recommendations, their recommendations fall into the following categories:

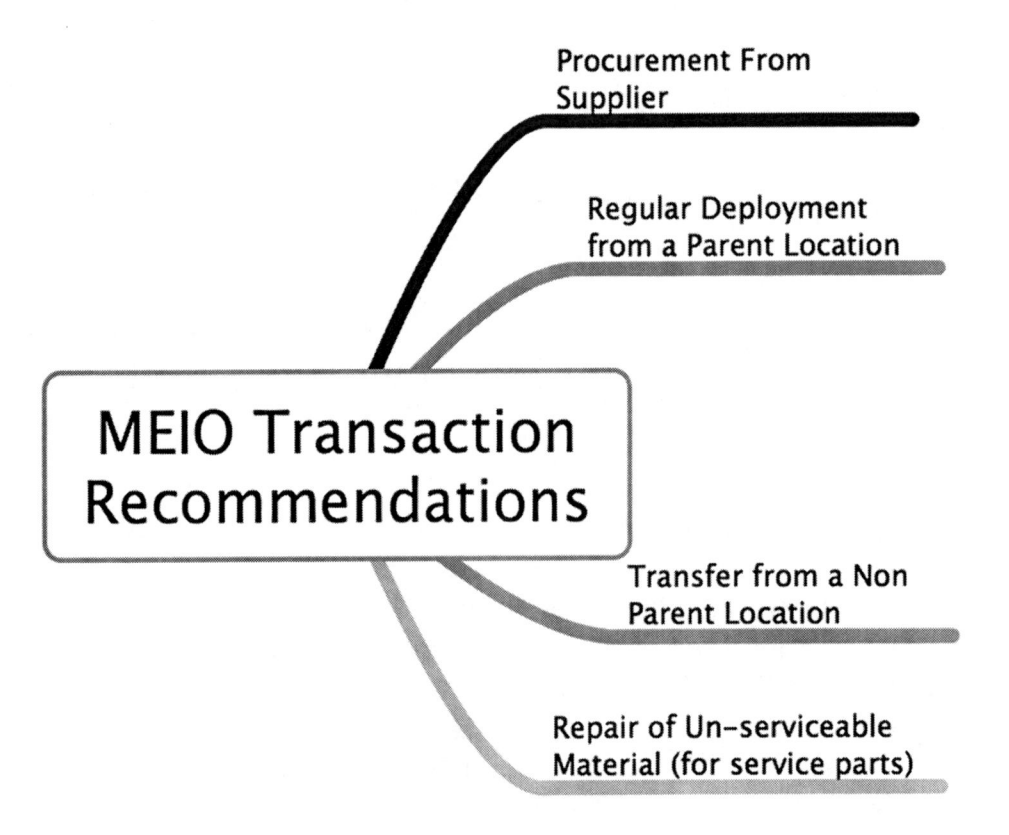

MEIO Transaction Recommendations
- Procurement From Supplier
- Regular Deployment from a Parent Location
- Transfer from a Non Parent Location
- Repair of Un-serviceable Material (for service parts)

Ranking the Recommendations Based on Impact

All MEIO applications perform ranking, but the approach is very different from non-MEIO methods of supply planning, which rely on a sequential approach of processing the product-location combinations in the supply network. Supply planning methods that take a sequential approach process one product-location combination after another until they have processed the entire supply network. Cost optimization divides the overall problem into a series of sub-problems based upon all locations that are valid for a particular product. This is called decomposition. For more on this topic see the post below:

http://www.scmfocus.com/sapplanning/2011/10/12/snp-optimizer-sub-problem-division-and-decomposition/

MEIO, on the other hand, works completely differently, and this feature is one of the very interesting aspects of MEIO. To make stocking decisions, it first calculates all the product locations together and then ranks them.

Insight into the Ranking

Servigistics provides extra visibility into the logic behind its ranking recommendations by actually displaying a detailed view of the logic in their interface. Their *Tactics Part Queue* provides a calculation for each procurement, repair or transfer order. It calculates the contribution for each recommendation and sorts the recommendations by those that offer the highest contribution to service levels. It is then a simple matter for the planner to focus on recommendations that will have the greatest impact on improving service levels.

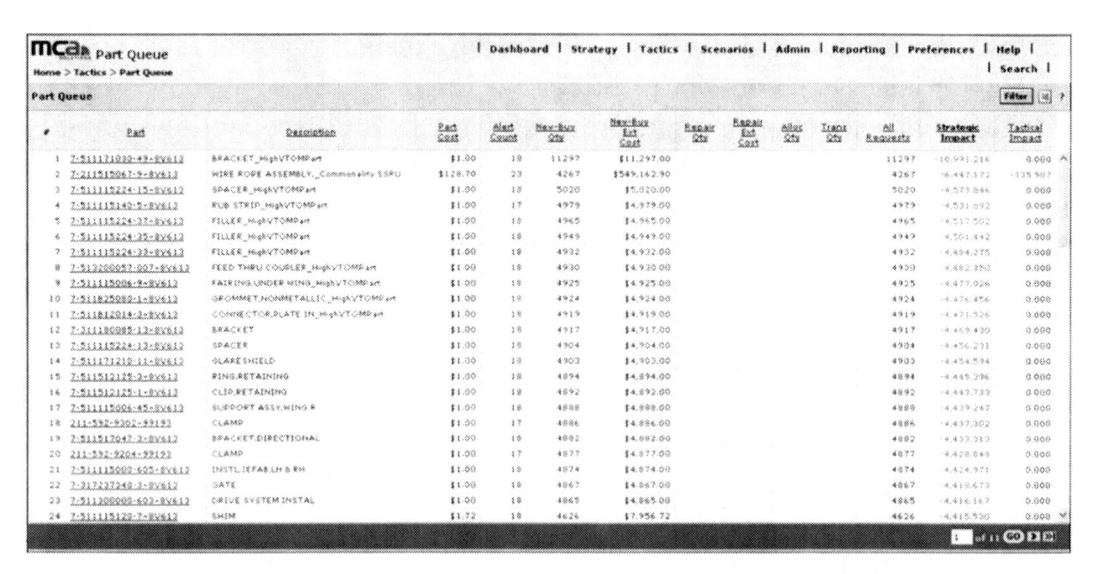

74   *Inventory Optimization and Multi-Echelon Planning Software*

This ranking view in Servigistics (formerly the MCA Solutions' application) shows which recommendations make the greatest contribution to service levels. These recommendations can also be viewed by category as you can see in the next screenshot. Notice the categories to the right.

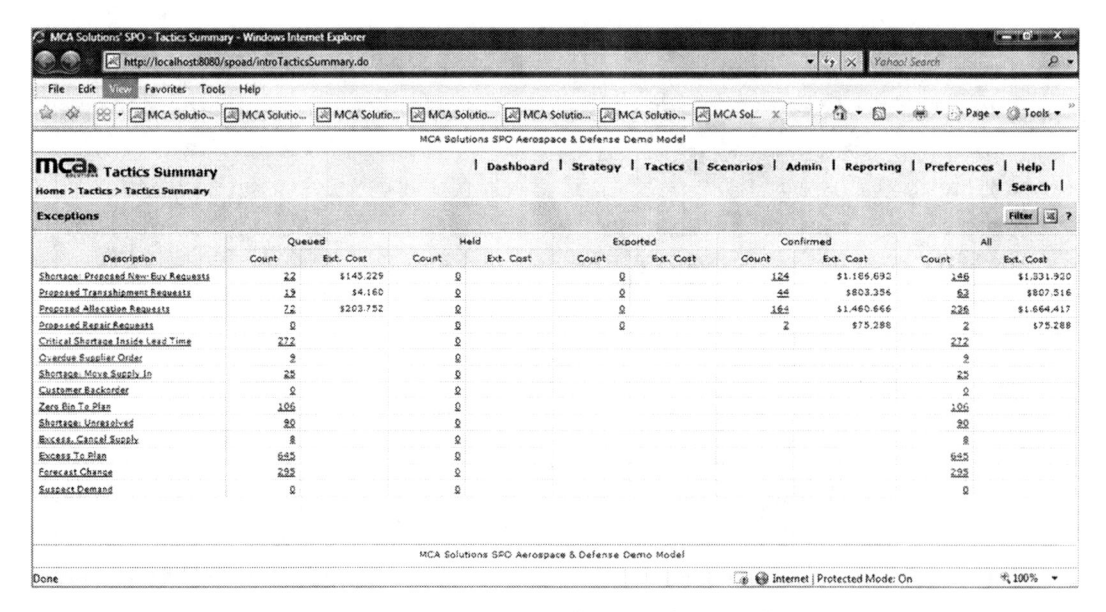

The Tactics Summary screen shows a count of each of the different types of alerts as well as transaction requests. Each category can then be selected and drilled into. This screen

also shows what is ready to be sent to the ERP system (Queued), what is held back (Held), and what was already sent (Exported).

Getting Alerts Right

In past consulting assignments, I have shown this screenshot to explain how alerts can be effectively integrated into a planning interface. I believe that integrating alerts in this manner is the best practice. It is part of Servigistics' *(formerly the MCA Solutions' application)* standard planning view and requires no configuration on the part of the application engineer. However, as soon as I write this, I know that product management at several vendors (not necessarily MEIO vendors, as I work across a variety of supply chain applications) will attempt to dilute my message about alerts. They will counter that their application also follows a best-practice in interface design by showing alerts in a pop-up window at the bottom of the screen. Alternatively, they will point out that one can navigate to a specialized alert transaction where all the alerts can be viewed. However, this is not what I am talking about; I am not referring to alerts than can appear in a separate screen, but to alerts that are integrated as part of the initial data view. In MCA's screen, nothing needs to "pop up" because the entire screen is an analytical screen and an alert screen combined into one.

Secondly, the alerts need to work right "out of the box," and need to continue working without troubleshooting. I work with a major vendor whose alerts occasionally stop working, or work only partially for some product-location combinations and not others, or appear in the main alert screen but not the main planning interface view. I am amazed that an enterprise application would have continual problems with alerts. However, it is a fact, and in addition to consuming support resources and funding, alerts that occasionally "go away" cause considerable concern with planners and reduce the buy-in to the system.

Exception-based Management Planning

Exception-based planning assumes that the system will make the majority of decisions correctly and that alerts will direct a planner's attention to significant items when necessary. However, many supply chain applications fall short of this goal in their design. In order to follow exception-based planning, two things are assumed:

1. A proper configuration of parameters and procedures between business and modeling requirements means that manual adjustments are infrequent.

2. Alerts are either preconfigured within the application or are easy to maintain through configuration changes.

The problem is that fewer companies than generally thought can follow exception-based management principles because the two preconditions for exception-based management exist in only a minority of supply chain planning applications.

Conclusion

MEIO is an innovative use of two separate forms of optimization: inventory optimization and multi-echelon optimization. Each answers separate supply chain planning questions. Inventory optimization answers the question of how much to keep in inventory, while multi-echelon optimization answers the question of where to keep inventory in the supply network. Unlike supply planning techniques that use sequential processing or calculation, MEIO calculates the service level impact of carrying one additional item at every product location combination and then sorts the list of options by their contribution to service levels and selects the best contributor. Different vendors do this in different ways, and during the software selection phase, it is worthwhile to understand how the vendors on your short-list perform this important step. MEIO applications do this for every stocking decision and iteratively build up the stock from the first stocking decision to the last, until it arrives at an ending stocking position. This ending stocking position, which is supported by a series of transaction recommendations, is then the "supply plan." This ending stock position is capped by either service levels or inventory investment targets. The best way to understand how this works is by using a simple and limited number of alternatives—as was described in the example earlier in this chapter—and then simply scaling up the problem mentally by the number of product-location combinations that will exist within the model. MEIO applications have to perform a service level contribution versus inventory cost calculation for every product-location combination for every inventory decision that is made. The complexity of the decision-making is impressive—and the more you understand the details of what MEIO is doing, the more impressive it appears.

CHAPTER 6

MEIO Versus Cost Optimization

How Inventory Optimization Differs from Cost Optimization
One of the most common questions regarding inventory optimization is how it differs from cost optimization. The answer is that inventory optimization and cost-based optimization are both mathematical optimizations. Cost optimization, where the objective function is to minimize costs, was the first method of optimization used in supply planning, and is in no way exclusive to supply chain planning. Inventory optimization, on the other hand, is relatively new and is exclusively used for supply planning. Therefore, cost optimization can be seen as a flexible form of optimization that applies to any environment for which costs can be estimated for various activities, while inventory optimization is customized and specific to supply planning.

When used for supply planning, a cost optimizer will require the estimation of a variety of costs that are incurred based upon different activities. Common costs include transportation, storage and stock-out costs, along with the costs of violating safety stock and of missed or unfulfilled demand. A MEIO optimizer also uses some of these costs, such as transportation and storage costs. When cost optimization is applied to other domains such as production planning, the cost categories that are used are completely different.

One thing that all cost optimizers have in common is the requirement for every activity to be broken down to a cost, because they can only interpret and act upon inputs that are declared as costs. This requirement is a frequent point of confusion because often tables that hold costs also hold things like durations. While the need for every activity to be broken down to a cost may be apparent to many readers, my experience in working with companies indicates that it is not at all apparent to everyone involved in the decisions of how to populate this data. Therefore, I want to be clear that in a cost optimizer, the durations are only used to calculate the time required to complete an activity, which declares to the system when material becomes available for the next process to be performed. However, the durations do not factor into the cost optimizer's decision-making. The cost optimizer literally cannot see anything but costs.

Cost Optimization Versus MEIO in Implementation

It is valuable to compare and contrast cost optimization to MEIO. I have always found that comparing and contrasting two or more related things to be one of the best ways of understanding each item individually. In this spirit I have created the following matrix, which compares each technology on criteria of interest.

	MEIO	Cost Optimization
Minimize Costs?	Yes to Inventory, No to Other	Yes
Strongly Control Service Level?	Yes	No
Constraint Based Planning?	No	Yes
Control over Production Order Frequency?	No	Yes
Redeployment?	Yes	No

	MEIO	**Cost Optimization**
Multiple Source Capability?	Yes, but Not Based Upon Production Constraints	Yes
The Ability to Calculate Across Stocking Locations?	Yes	No

This matrix is designed to provide some insight into the major differences in functionality between cost optimization and MEIO. There is no perfect matrix to instantly explain all of the differences between the two methods. Furthermore, one of the most difficult areas to represent is the probability of each different functionality area being implemented successfully, and I do not have probabilities of success listed on the graphic above. Generally a great deal of emphasis is placed upon whether a method or particular vendor has the desired functionality, and much less emphasis on how likely it is that the functionality will be taken live. Cost optimization has the widest potential functionality set of the above methods, but also the lowest likelihood of success. Secondly, companies differ in their funding levels and capabilities with respect to IT, IT support, master data maintenance and supply chain planning. Some methods require that more capabilities be implemented than others, so the evaluation of both the supply planning method and vendor must be performed within the context of the company's abilities. This is another factor not included in the graphic above.

More on the probability of success of different APS methods can be found here:

http://www.scmfocus.com/supplyplanning/2011/07/17/considering-the-probability-of-success-of-different-aps-methods-for-supply-planning/

The Importance of Understanding Cost Optimization

Understanding cost optimization is important to understanding and implementing MEIO for several reasons.

1. MEIO and cost optimization are the only methods of supply planning that use optimization to create the supply plan.

2. They present similar challenges in terms of complexity, the necessity for thorough explanation and thorough solution socialization.

3. As pointed out earlier, both cost optimization and MEIO use costs, although cost optimization uses costs in its objective function. Cost optimization requires the setting of penalty costs, which are implicit costs and more difficult to estimate than explicit costs. Both optimization methods use explicit costs and both methods share a number of the challenges of cost estimation.

4. Cost optimization preceded MEIO and has had many more implementations and attempts at implementation. However, cost optimization continues to run into a number of problems. Those desiring to implement MEIO can learn from these challenges.

In this section, I will cover how cost optimization works in theory and how cost optimizers are generally implemented. The way cost optimizers work technically is covered in a wide variety of printed materials. However, I think that the coverage of how cost optimizers for supply planning are implemented in practice is new, aside from case studies that have a primarily positive spin, as I have not found anything similar in the academic articles and books that I have reviewed on cost optimization. Wikipedia seems to agree with my assessment with respect to cost optimization.

> Secondly, the techniques are claimed to be commercially effective. The companies publish case studies that show how clients have achieved reductions in inventory whilst maintaining or improving availability. There is limited published data outside of these case studies, and a reluctance for some practitioners to publish details of their successes (which may be commercially sensitive), therefore, hard evidence is difficult to come by.

However, I must provide a counterpoint on the Wikipedia entry: If practitioners are reticent to publish successes, they are much more reticent to publish failures or even areas where they made mistakes. In fact, publicly traded companies cannot publish failures because failures can reduce the stock price of companies. Enormous financial incentives exist to prevent truthful but unflattering information from ever falling into the public realm. This means that companies that published major success stories about their software implementations, which in turn are used in vendor marketing literature, may have in fact failed absolutely or failed to meet expectations. Talking to someone who has worked on the project is the only way to discover the truth. In fact, the only reason I can publish this is that I work as an independent consultant. We learn the most when the truth is published; however, the truth is often less appealing than marketing fantasy and the truth does not always maximize profits. Because the majority of information available on enterprise software is generally commercial in nature, we have a system of publication that is very biased toward perpetuating fantasy over reality.

What is Cost Optimization?

Generally speaking, when cost optimizers are discussed in the context of supply planning projects they are often simply referred to as "optimizers." I find it more descriptive to further define an optimizer in terms of its objective function, which is based upon its goal. This is not to say that other optimizers with non-cost objective functions do not use costs at all. However, the difference is that they do not use costs as part of the objective function. What the objective function is minimizing or maximizing is one of the best categorization methods that I can think of.

Using this nomenclature on projects is beneficial because this keeps project team members oriented around what the optimizer is driving toward. It helps keep the contingent of the team that is not deeply involved with the optimizer from presuming that the optimizer is optimizing factors such as duration that are not in fact part of the optimizer's goal.

How Cost Optimization Works

In planning the supply network, cost optimization assumes that costs are the overriding driver of the supply chain, and that the goal of the supply chain organization is to minimize costs. To do so, the cost optimizer requires that all costs be defined in the model. These costs are both explicit (such as transportation costs) and implicit or penalty (such as the costs of unfulfilled demand). Cost optimizers then trade the costs off against one another by initiating the major recommendations (purchase, production, repair [for service parts], and stock transfer recommendations) in such a way that total costs are minimized. Cost optimization can be continuous—with much of the reality of the supply chain removed and resulting in short solve times—or discrete, which includes things like lot sizes and longer solve times.

With cost optimization, actual penalty costs can never entirely be entered into the model. One reason for this is that if only the direct costs associated with a lost sale were entered as the unfulfilled demand cost, the service level would be too low to meet the company's objectives. This is explained in more detail in the post below:

http://www.scmfocus.com/supplyplanning/2011/07/24/why-the-cost-of-missed-demand-must-alway-be-set-so-much-higher-than-the-profit-margin/

This is just one reason among several as to why costs cannot be set to actual costs and why the total cost values that are calculated by cost optimization runs are not useful in understanding the actual costs of the supply plan. Instead, the costs are only useful in comparing one run against other runs to obtain a comparative reading on, for instance, whether a change to a master data parameter causes total costs to increase or decrease. In fact, the most common way to set up costs in cost optimizers for supply planning is to overwhelming emphasize the costs of unfulfilled demand, or what translates very roughly to a service level goal. What is often not considered is that cost optimization can only seek to minimize the penalty costs of missed customer orders. For instance, a penalty cost for a missed customer order may be set at fifty times greater than the cost of violating safety stock. However, that does not approximate to any particular service level. What can be said is that the service level will be high in this scenario, because the cost of stocking out is so high relative to the cost of fulfilling from inventory. Of course, the service level attained may be too high and too expensive for the company to reasonably be expected to stock.

The Understanding and General Availability of Supply Chain Costs

Something that took me quite some time to understand is that companies do not have a good grasp of their implicit or explicit supply chain costs. I am as surprised as anyone would be at this revelation, and if I did not have first-hand experience seeing this at multiple companies I would not believe it. Books on this topic certainly don't talk about this fact. In fact, most books tend to make the assumption that cost gathering regularly takes place, and all that is necessary is to place the costs into the model.

Furthermore, the issue of limited cost information is not restricted to supply planning but is also true of the other supply chain domains where cost optimization is used. Unlike cost information, companies can readily provide their inventory investment budgets and their service level goals, even if only at a high level. However, when service levels need to be fleshed out to a more detailed level, companies invariably run into political debates as to what part of the business or section of the product database is more important than other parts. However, the fact that there are heated debates on service levels means that at least the participants understand the implications of this setting.

This level of understanding is not normally the case with the implicit penalty costs (i.e., the cost of unfulfilled demand, safety stock violation and shelf life). Implicit costs, which are required in order to populate cost optimizers, are the most difficult to estimate. Penalty costs are not used in MEIO, which in my view is one reason as to why costs are often set arbitrarily in these cost optimizers.

I once analyzed the configuration of a client's production planning and scheduling system. Based on this analysis, I pointed out that while the changeover durations were populated, there were no changeover costs. (Changeover is activity of switching the manufacturing line to produce a different product. High changeover costs promote longer production runs, while lower changeover costs promote shorter production runs.) I told my client that I thought this was a serious issue because the cost optimizer they were using performed the solve using costs, not durations. (Durations were there only to allow the system to calculate how long it would take to complete the changeover and thus to calculate the manufacturing lead time, and were not used to drive the optimizer's decisions.) I was asked if simply multiplying the duration by a consistent factor of one dollar per minute to arrive at costs could solve this problem. To this I responded that while their proposal would certainly let the system perform the solve, it would not be correct, and it was not the way to set up a system of this type. Unfortunately this conversation occurred right before the company wanted to go live rather than early in the design process when a conversation of this nature should take place. This company simply had no understanding that first, costs needed to be entered in order for the system to work properly, and secondly, that their business team for the project should have determined both costs and durations separately to approximate their actual costs and durations. This along with countless other experiences has left me with little doubt that service levels are more tangible to companies than costs.

The second major issue with setting costs is that no one explains to companies how cost optimization works beyond the basics, nor do companies spend much time or effort themselves trying to understand how to set costs properly. I have witnessed companies using the most unsupportable cost structures in optimizers because the costs that were initially set were those that "sort of gave desirable output." In addition, the cost structure was adopted because an expert from a software vendor signed off on it! That was the extent of the work that was done to validate costs. Not documenting the logic behind the costs that are placed into optimizers is also not uncommon.

Some implementing companies have a strong tendency to allow their IT departments to take control of cost setting. I have observed this poor implementation strategy, which companies should be careful to avoid. Allowing the IT department to take control of cost setting is a problem because the business needs to own cost setting and must invest the time to understand the optimizer. Running the optimizer is an IT function, but the determination of costs and other business logic settings is not. It makes a lot of sense for the master data team to be responsible for physically making changes to the costs, as costs are technically part of master data. However, only the business has the logic, or can develop the logic for what the costs should be and they should not delegate this responsibility to IT. Secondly IT should not try to assume the responsibility of setting costs to increase its level of control, nor should it be delegated to the software vendor. The vendor can provide input and examples of what they have seen at other companies, but the ultimate decision resides with the business. This is why graphics like the one below are important to reference on projects. It is critical to build an understanding within the business of how the costs work together to create various outcomes.

The Effect of Increasing Different Costs on the Frequency of Production Orders

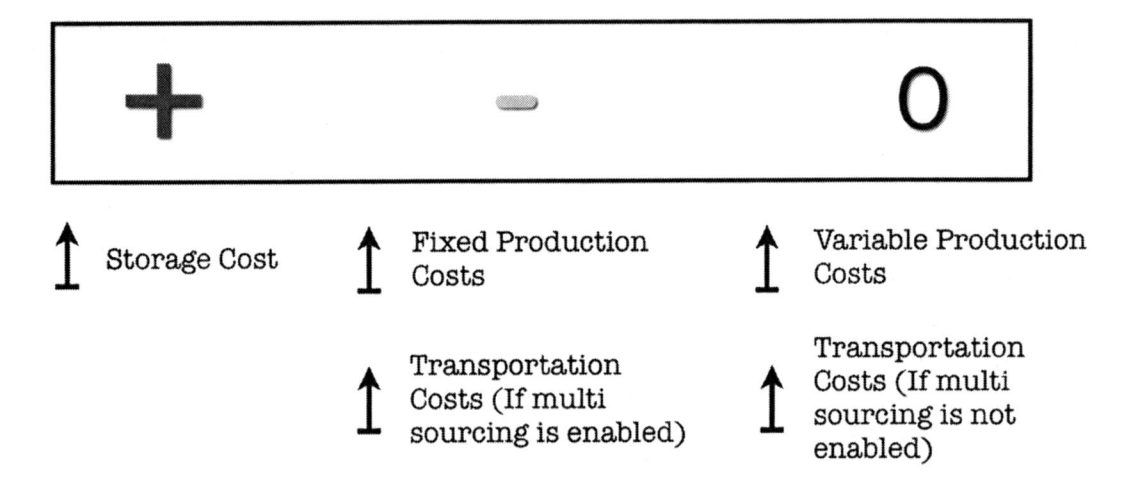

| + | − | 0 |

↕ Storage Cost

↕ Fixed Production Costs

↕ Transportation Costs (If multi sourcing is enabled)

↕ Variable Production Costs

↕ Transportation Costs (If multi sourcing is not enabled)

The reality of implementing cost optimization is either not documented or is lightly documented in books and other written sources. There is a strong tendency, I believe, to publish information on the potential of a technology rather than on the reality. This is particularly true in the enterprise software market where a lot of money is at stake and the interpretation of the success of various projects directly influences careers. However, the fact is that while executives want to "optimize" their supply chain, and want to perform both constraint-based planning and multi-sourcing, once a company makes the decision to use a cost optimizer, in most cases, they are unsure how to use it. This situation is unlikely to change until businesses understand cost optimization and adjustments are made to the implementation methodology for cost optimization projects.

The Common Problems of Cost Optimization

I have seen a number of optimization clients in my consulting work, and it is clear that several easy-to-identify factors have limited the benefits of cost optimization projects. When I triangulate my experience with the experience of others involved in similar projects, there is little debate as to the common problems with cost optimization. Here are the issues:

1. It is very difficult to agree on what costs should be entered into the optimization model. This is true regardless of the fact that real costs are not even required for cost-based optimization. Only relative costs are necessary, and these costs simply declare the relative cost weights that should be applied to different supply chain activities (e.g., if carrying costs are set to "1" and a transportation lane cost is set to "2," these are not "real" costs; in fact they are not even proportionately accurate). It is quite common, or may in fact be the norm, to set non-proportional costs for the explicit costs (my sample is not large enough to say for sure). The implicit costs (the costs for which the company does not get a bill, such as the cost of missing a demand) are set even more arbitrarily. They are not set proportionally to the explicit costs, nor are they set with a firm grounding in the goals of the company. Sloppy and unsubstantiated cost setting is often explained by the fact that the company was not sure what to enter, so changes were made to the costs until the output looked "about right."

2. How cost categories incur costs and how they aggregate and influence decision-making by the optimizer are often not well understood. For instance, the variable cost of production is incurred once when the product is produced, but storage costs are incurred for every day the item is held in inventory. Therefore, each cost has a very different incidence of accumulation and contribution to the overall cost. It is not sufficient to simply compare production costs to storage costs without understanding how they are accumulated. However, mistakes like this are quite common.

3. Companies often have difficulty maintaining their explicit cost data (cost for which there is a record to check against). I have found it relatively easy to find errors in the costs used by a company to drive optimization results. These costs may be driving the solution for years before the problem is brought to the company's attention.

4. Cost optimization results are more difficult to explain than those of other methods. If the costs are not within a close proximity to actual costs in

relative terms, the model will produce strange results, causing some supply chain professionals to distrust the results of cost-based optimization.

5. In implementation, cost optimization appears to have problems adapting to changes in the business. This gets back to the high "encapsulation" of the optimizer with respect to costs and the fact that it can frequently be interpreted as a black box. Again, the costs are abstractions that drive decisions. They are only understood by a small number of people in the company, if by anyone at all. Once set, planners are not given responsibility for changing the optimization costs. As previously stated, more often than not this role is given to IT, which makes little sense as IT cannot tell the business what the right costs should be. Therefore, while the costs may (I say may, because they often don't) reflect the priorities of the company at the time of implementation, costs and company priorities change over time. While priorities change, the optimizer often ends up stuck in the past because companies have so many problems maintaining the controlling factors of cost optimization software.

6. Although cost optimization does not absolutely need to have resource constraints—or to be planned in a finite manner—finite planning is one of the major selling points of optimization. Companies that have no particular interest in cost optimization often select cost optimization for its ability to perform two things: multi-sourcing and constraint-based or finite planning. All of the cost optimization projects I have worked on have at least attempted to perform constraint-based planning. However, constraint-based planning projects have their own issues related to master data accuracy, and the problems and complexity with constraint-based planning end up being co-mingled and add to the standard problems of cost optimization. Furthermore, I have yet to see a company that correctly estimates the amount of effort required for their constraint-based planning project, and the amount of effort placed into maintaining resource accuracy is significantly underestimated. The complexities and challenges of constraint-based planning projects are independent of the supply planning method used, but they place an additional load on the project. Projects that select

allocation, as the supply planning method and that use finite resources are much more challenging than allocation projects that are implemented with unconstrained resources.

Constraint-based Planning

I treat constraint-based planning much more substantially in the book, *Supply Planning with MRP, DRP and APS Software*. However, it is important to discuss it briefly here because it is an important component of cost optimization software.

I have discussed how MEIO applications differ from one another and how important it is for the company to understand these differences in order to select the right MEIO software for its needs. There are also key design differences between the major supply planning methods. Cost optimization and allocation applications typically allow for constraint-based planning, while MRP, DRP, heuristics and MEIO do not. The constraint-based planning that is explained as part of cost optimization and allocation is often assumed to include supply planning constraints such as transportation capacity, storage capacity, etc. However, these are not the constraints that are set up and used in the vast majority of cost optimization and allocation supply planning implementations. To see more about the types of resources that are included in supply planning systems see the following post:

http://www.scmfocus.com/supplyplanning/2011/10/02/commonly-used-and-unused-constraints-for-supply-planning/

Production resources are the most commonly constrained resources in supply planning systems, although they are less detailed than the production resources that are entered into production planning systems. Someone might ask why this is the case, and it is quite a good question. The reason for this is that the concept of using and constraining resources does not apply as well to supply planning as it does to production planning. Constraint-based planning actually began in production planning and scheduling, and then migrated over to supply planning. However, supply planning and production planning are significantly different. For example, not all, but many production resources are frequently part of a production line where the overall production line pace can be set and constrained by a single bottleneck resource. To read more about finite and bottleneck resources see this post:

http://www.scmfocus.com/sapplanning/2009/07/01/bottleneck-resources/

However, by including production resources in a supply planning system, the software solution is essentially given a dual purpose: the application creates both the supply plan and the initial production plan. For simple production scheduling environments, an application specifically for production planning and scheduling may not be necessary. This is covered in the post below:

http://www.scmfocus.com/productionplanningandscheduling/2011/03/29/why-mixing-operations-can-be-appropriate-for-weak-production-scheduling-applications/

However, more complex and detailed production planning environments use specific applications to perform production planning and scheduling. These environments require more detail than can be provided by a supply planning application that is constrained by production resources and that creates the initial production plan.

In terms of functionality comparison, the fact that cost optimization applications normally have the ability to constrain on production resources, while MEIO does not, leads to the next topic: leveraging the use of production constraints in order to switch sourcing locations when necessary. This functionality is called multi-sourcing.

Multi-Sourcing in Cost Optimization versus MEIO

Multi-sourcing is the ability of the supply planning system to flexibly pull supply from two or more locations.[2] Two things are required to perform multi-sourcing:

1. The valid location-to-location combinations must be set up in the master data. For example, if Location C and Location B can supply Location A, then the system must see the relationship between the locations.

2. The system must have the ability to choose different source locations. This logic allows the system to choose between the locations when given different scenarios.

The ultimate goal is for the system to automatically adjust the selected source of supply based upon such factors as stock availability or capacity at each location.

Multi-sourcing works off of two basic scenarios: a stock limitation scenario and a production limitation scenario.

- In the stock limitation scenario, when a source location does not have stock, the system simply has to provide stock from the source location where it is available. Both cost optimization and MEIO can do this.

- Cost optimization enterprise applications often are built to have production constraints. In the production limitation scenario, cost optimization can—if the necessary configuration is performed—switch to a different source location to plan the supply. MEIO applications do not currently incorporate production constraints, so they cannot substitute a second location on the basis of production capacity.

The ability of cost optimization software to respond to multi-sourcing production limitations is often noted as a reason for selecting cost optimization software. However, in practice multi-sourcing is seldom executed effectively, and this point is not emphasized adequately. Beyond the technical complexity, multi-sourcing in cost optimization software results in much longer run times than a single-sourcing

---

[2] Multi-sourcing is actually a better-known term in IT and relates to the outsourcing of IT services to multiple vendors. However, I am using the term here in its lesser-known definition as it relates to supply planning.

configuration. This is because the problem, or search space, becomes much larger when the optimizer is required to take multiple sourcing locations into account. The actual complexity of implementing cost optimization—with all of the bells and whistles demonstrated in sales presentations—is rarely written about, giving the wrong impression as to the general effectiveness of cost optimization. In my project experience with multi-sourcing in cost optimization projects, the functionality is rarely enabled.

Synthetizing the Multitude of Reasons for the Limited Success of Cost Optimization
The fact is that cost-based optimization has not been successfully implemented in many companies. There are numerous reasons for this lack of success, including those listed above and those that I explore in a separate book on cost optimization, titled *Supply Planning with MRP, DRP, and APS Software*. The senior executives who approved the funding for optimization would be surprised as to how far most companies are from a solution that is superior over older supply chain planning methods.

Implementation of cost-based optimization could be greatly improved. However, implementing companies, software vendors and consulting firms are unwilling to share information on the problems they have faced with implementing cost optimization. This restricts the ability of decision makers—both at companies that have implemented cost optimization and those that wish to do so—from gaining the necessary information to adjust their implementation methodology.

Will the Same Thing that Happened to Cost Optimization Happen to MEIO?

One of the jokes in the advanced planning space is that "you sell optimization, but go live with heuristics," which begs the question: "Will MEIO face the same fate?" MEIO is quite different than the methods that supply chain professionals know and are acclimated to using. This works against the adoption of MEIO, as the greater the gap between what people know and what they don't know, the more training that is required. So on this count MEIO faces a similar challenge as cost optimization. However, in another area, MEIO has a significant advantage over cost optimization, and it may not face the same fate. Inventory optimization is a more structured way of performing optimization, and it is customized for supply planning in a way that cost optimization never was. For this and other reasons, including some of the advancements in usability and understandability, I predict a better outcome for MEIO than cost optimization. However, don't use this reason as an excuse not to perform the necessary background research to become educated about mis-steps on previous cost optimization and MEIO projects. By doing this research, a repetition of the same mistakes can be prevented.

Cost Minimization, Service Level Control and Common Supply Planning Objectives

Companies certainly want to minimize their costs. However, there is quite a bit more to supply planning than simply meeting all demands while minimizing costs. This is doubly true when one observes how supply planning is performed in companies (this topic is covered in Chapter 6: "MEIO Versus Cost Optimization"). Cost optimizers simply don't work the way the majority of people who work at arm's length with them think they work. First, cost optimizers do not have an inherent concept of service levels. Instead, they have the concept of a penalty cost for an unfulfilled demand (i.e., a lost sale). An important consideration is that all costs in a cost optimizer only make sense in relation to one another. The company that intends to use cost optimization must develop a penalty cost for an unfulfilled demand, and this penalty cost must appropriately reflect how that company values the unfulfilled demand versus the cost of violating safety stock. However, what is that cost? It is very difficult to place a firm value on this. The penalty cost is not simply the lost profit of the product, because there are other considerations, such as the reputation of the company in the customer's mind and competitive concerns. The list of things to consider is quite lengthy. This has been known for some time, as pointed out by George Plossl in 1985:

> An equally difficult problem arises when an attempt is made to determine out-of-stock costs. Customer dissatisfaction with back orders may be very costly, but it is difficult—if not impossible—to assign a specific value to it with any degree of accuracy. One back order may cause little or no customer inconvenience, while the next may be the reason that the customer buys elsewhere in the future. The stock out

cost, like the inventory carrying cost, is an artificial concept demanded by the mathematical formulas which have been derived to assist in making inventory decisions.

The result of all of this is that getting to a solid penalty cost number is extremely challenging and the company can never be sure of the relationship between this number and the service level.

The unfulfilled demand penalty cost is simply a convenient way to get the optimizer to consider a concept of service and is not a term often used by the business. Therefore, cost optimizers essentially speak a different language from the business. This language requires translation, which often leads to a mistranslation of the business needs to the system's settings.

Nevertheless, the business does speak the language of service levels. Service levels and inventory investment are generally much more concrete and easier to add into a model. But, companies only loosely understand the relationship between service levels and costs, which is why so many unattainable service level goals exist. When used and socialized properly, the MEIO application can cut through the confusion between service levels and inventory costs by making the relationship clear and at least providing the potential for improving the way in which companies set this metric.

Optimization with specific service level targets is, of course, the design of MEIO applications. All of the other methods only *approximately* control service levels and leave the supply chain organization with imprecise controls over the attained service level. The less precise the control, the more manual effort is required to adjust the plan to achieve the desired outcomes. This precision of control over the important factors for supply planning organizations is a main reason inventory optimization has so much potential to change the planning and control of supply networks.

MEIO Versus Cost Optimization 95

						Total SKUs: 6		Total Locations: 5		Total Items: 10	
Forward Horizon: 24 Months			Total Demand ($/Month)		Total Demand (Units/Month)		On-Hand Inventory Investment ($)		On-Hand Inventory (Units)	
	Proposed		$645,787		32,498		$238,497		10,359	
	In-Production		$703,117		33,472		$400,156		13,979	
	Difference		($57,330)		-974		($161,659)		-3,621	

Item Navigation

Item	Select	Location	SKU	SKU Description	Accept/Reject	Safety Stock (Days)	Exception Count	Average Demand (Units/Month)	Demand Uncertainty (%/Month)	Service Level (%)	Lead Time (Days)	On-Hand Inventory (Days)	On-Hand Inventory Investment ($)
Details	☐	RDC1	SP24	FG Product 24		8.7	1	30,485	26%		1	8.7	$165,674
Details	☐	NDC	SP21	FG Product 21		48.4	1	909	95%		2	51.5	$70,054
Details	☐	V2	RM2	Raw Material Type 2		11.8	4	774	47%		9	11.8	$2,081
Details	☐	RDC3	SP25	FG Product 25		7.8	1	31	40%	95.0%	1	7.8	$174
Details	☐	RDC2	SP25	FG Product 25		7.4	1	31	40%		1	7.4	$167
Details	☐	NDC	RM2	Raw Material Type 2		1.8	1	225	50%		0	1.8	$93
Details	☐	NDC	SP29	FG Product 29		7.7	1	13	43%		2	10.8	$83
Details	☐	RDC1	SP29	FG Product 29		7.4	2	13	43%	95.0%	1	7.4	$81
Details	☐	RDC3	SP28	FG Product 28		7.8	2	11	45%	95.0%	1	7.8	$52
Details	☐	NDC	SP28	FG Product 28		10.4	1	6	50%		2	13.9	$37

This view from Logility's Voyager Inventory Optimization demonstrates the type of control over service levels that is available with MEIO software. The service level per item is apparent, as well as other important statistics, such as the lead-time, on-hand inventory, and inventory investment.

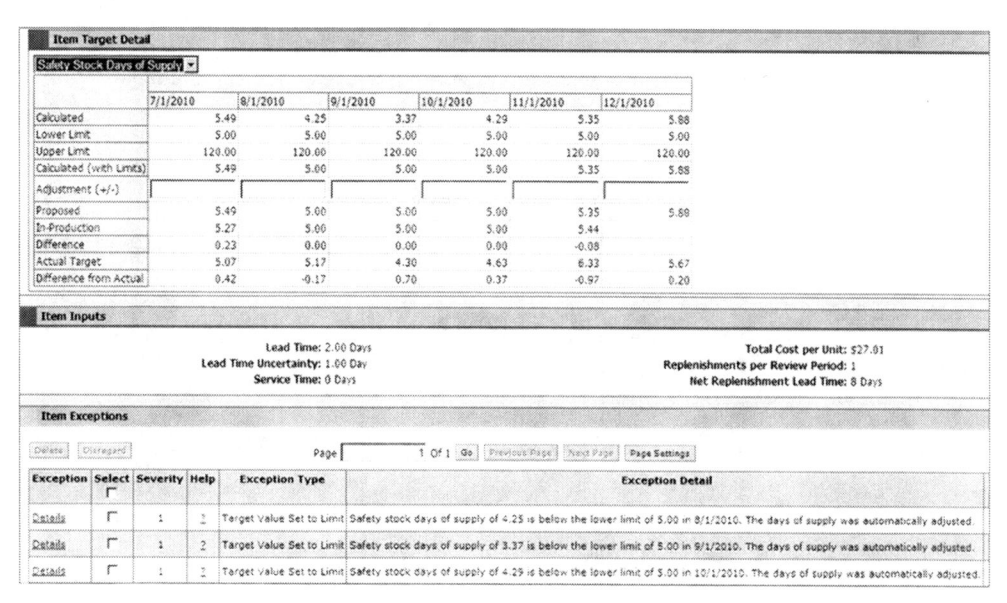

Item Target Detail

Safety Stock Days of Supply

	7/1/2010	8/1/2010	9/1/2010	10/1/2010	11/1/2010	12/1/2010
Calculated	5.49	4.25	3.37	4.29	5.35	5.88
Lower Limit	5.00	5.00	5.00	5.00	5.00	5.00
Upper Limit	120.00	120.00	120.00	120.00	120.00	120.00
Calculated (with Limits)	5.49	5.00	5.00	5.00	5.35	5.88
Adjustment (+/-)						
Proposed	5.49	5.00	5.00	5.00	5.35	5.88
In-Production	5.27	5.00	5.00	5.00	5.44	
Difference	0.23	0.00	0.00	0.00	-0.08	
Actual Target	5.07	5.17	4.30	4.63	6.33	5.67
Difference from Actual	0.42	-0.17	0.70	0.37	-0.97	0.20

Item Inputs

Lead Time: 2.00 Days
Lead Time Uncertainty: 1.00 Day
Service Time: 0 Days

Total Cost per Unit: $27.01
Replenishments per Review Period: 1
Net Replenishment Lead Time: 8 Days

Item Exceptions

Exception	Select	Severity	Help	Exception Type	Exception Detail
Details	☐	1	?	Target Value Set to Limit	Safety stock days of supply of 4.25 is below the lower limit of 5.00 in 8/1/2010. The days of supply was automatically adjusted.
Details	☐	1	?	Target Value Set to Limit	Safety stock days of supply of 3.37 is below the lower limit of 5.00 in 9/1/2010. The days of supply was automatically adjusted.
Details	☐	1	?	Target Value Set to Limit	Safety stock days of supply of 4.29 is below the lower limit of 5.00 in 10/1/2010. The days of supply was automatically adjusted.

A screen opens for any selected product, which displays more information specific to the product. This is the Inventory Policy Tab of the item, which allows the user to make the desired adjustments.

Service Level Setting and the Service Level Hierarchy

Along with different types of optimization, there are different approaches to inventory optimization, as reflected in the variety of vendor applications available. The more time spent analyzing the software of different MEIO vendors, the more I am struck by these design differences. One of the most important areas of differentiation is where the service level is set in the software. This is described in the graphic below.

Degree of Service Level Control

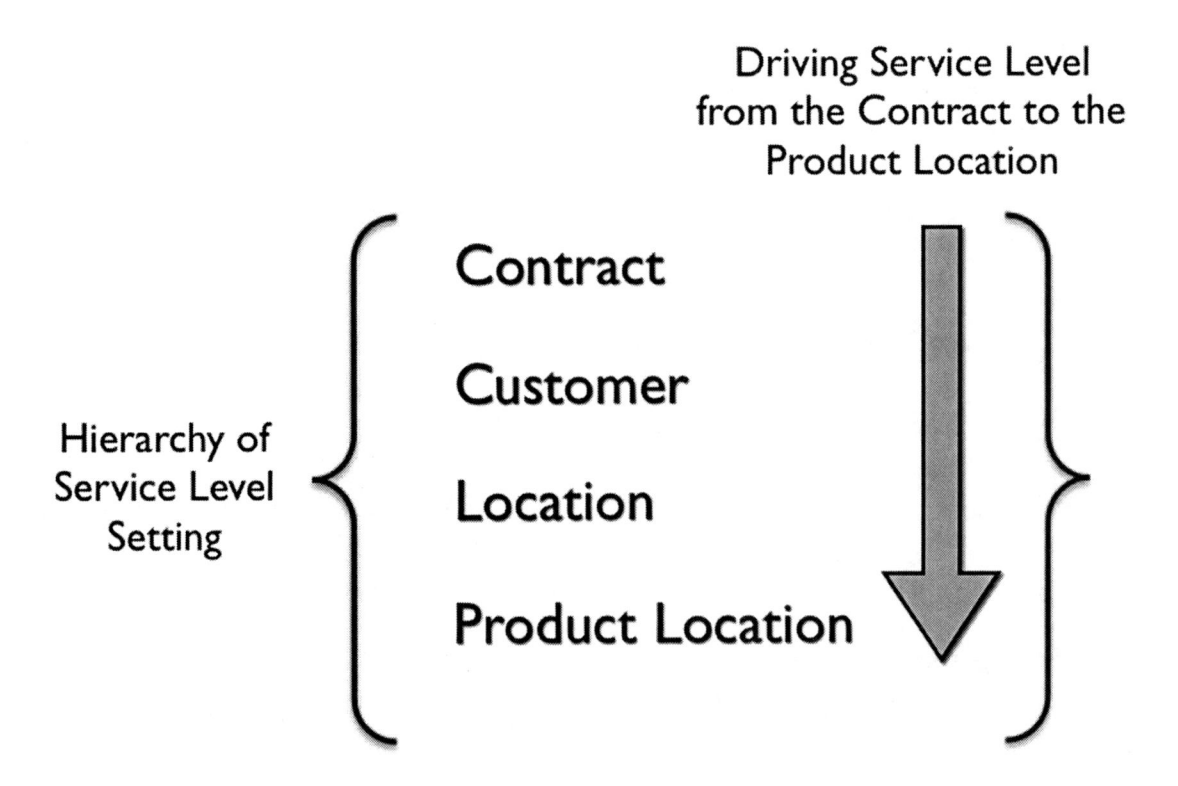

Hierarchy of Service Level Setting:
- Contract
- Customer
- Location
- Product Location

Driving Service Level from the Contract to the Product Location

Where the service level can be set in the application makes a very big difference in terms of how the company can use the application as well as how powerful the application is, but also in the degree of maintenance required after the application is installed. MEIO applications can be categorized partially by how easily the service level is set and how high in the hierarchy—contract, customer, location, and product location—the service level can be set (this is covered in more detail in Chapter 4: "Multi-Echelon Planning Explained"). However, what I perceive as the best way is certainly not how all companies want their supply plan managed. Some companies only want to define the service level at the product location and will never set service levels at the customer. At this point, a MEIO application can be found and configured for every approach to setting service levels. More detail on where service levels are controlled in MEIO applications is available at the post below:

http://www.scmfocus.com/inventoryoptimizationmultiechelon/2010/01/inventory-optimization-flexibility-and-the-service-level-hierarchy/

Conclusion

Inventory optimization is different from cost optimization. Whereas cost optimization is focused on minimizing the supply chain costs, inventory optimization is built around the relationship between service level and inventory investment—the fundamental reason for implementing MEIO software. Stating goals in terms of service level and inventory investment is more natural for companies than attempting to estimate penalty costs.

How MEIO compares to cost optimization was explored in this chapter. MEIO, in spite of the effort needed for the initial implementation, requires less maintenance than other methods of supply planning, primarily because of its ability to provide precise control of the supply plan in a way that matches the main key performance indicators of the business. However, cost optimization has the ability to perform constraint-based planning (where the predominant resource constraints tend to be production not supply planning), and because of this, most cost optimization applications can also perform multi-sourcing if the application is configured properly. Significantly older than MEIO, cost optimization has many more implementations globally; however, it has also been a risky supply planning implementation method. It is recommended that companies that want to implement either cost optimization or MEIO learn from the mistakes of others by putting effort into learning the history of cost optimization. Many of these mistakes have been explained in this chapter. If this is done, MEIO need not replicate the relatively low success rate of cost optimization projects. MEIO has several advantages over cost optimization, one prominent advantage being that service levels and inventory investment are already part of the common language of supply chain departments, while penalty costs are not.

At a high level of abstraction, MEIO is philosophically intuitive in many ways. But when one gets into the details, it becomes evident that the effort required to educate businesses about MEIO is comparable to cost optimization. As with cost optimization, MEIO's assumptions diverge from the supply planning methods with which most supply chain planning professionals are familiar. A lack of education in cost optimization has been the Achilles heel of the implementation of this supply planning method, and I have already witnessed several examples of similar problems of improper solution socialization on MEIO projects. Therefore, education is something to focus on in future MEIO implementations.

CHAPTER 7

MEIO and Simulation

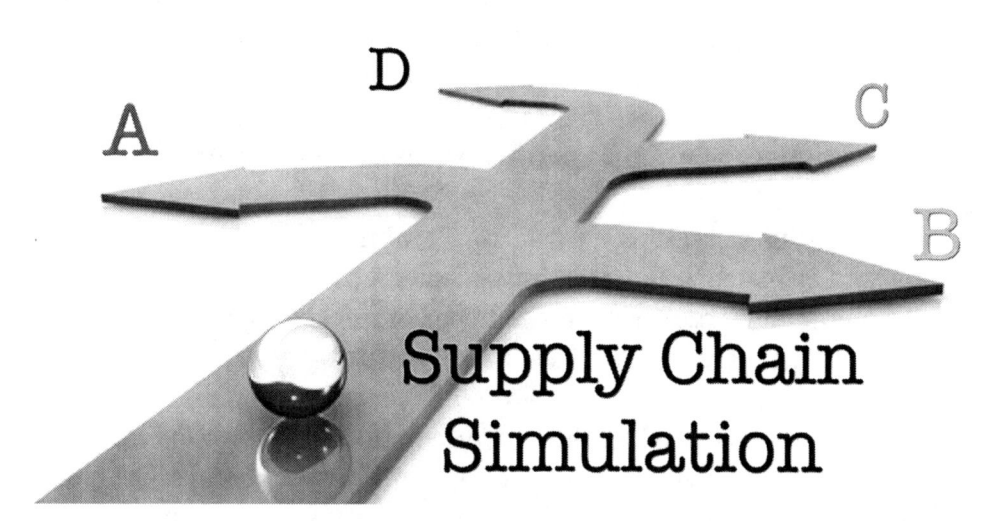

Much underutilized by supply chain organizations, supply planning simulation can allow companies to select from any number of alternative service levels, inventory investments and controlling parameters. Simulation is a real strength of many MEIO applications.

What is Simulation?

The following definition of software simulation from Wikipedia has some interesting implications for planning software.

> Simulation software is based on the process of modeling a real phenomenon with a set of mathematical formulas. It is, essentially, a program that allows the user to observe an operation through simulation without actually performing that operation. Simulation software is used widely to design equipment so that the final product will be as close to design specs as possible without expensive in-process modification.

First, I want to make sure to differentiate software simulation from simulation as a method of problem solving. Simulation, such as simulated annealing, is a heuristic approach to solving what is typically an optimization problem that has a very large solution space (i.e., a difficult problem to solve). Therefore, the simulation that we will cover here is where the MEIO solution analyzes the planning results from changes to the system using different sets of master data.

Secondly, planning software itself is related to simulation because a planning system does not actually execute the recommendations that it makes. Planning system results are changed by planners in the hopes of improving the recommendations that are sent to the ERP system. A supply planning system works off of a forecast, which will always have some degree of inaccuracy, so a supply plan is a projection, or a best guess of what the recommendations should be. Making slight or major changes to the setup and the assumptions of the system could generate multiple supply plans. Which of the various setups results in the best supply planning performance will be known only after the fact, and any company would naturally desire to be able to compare different setups used in the past, find the best one, and use it in the future.

That is the concept behind simulation. Simulation is essentially a disciplined way of running scenarios in a planning system, where each scenario is different from the main production or "live" scenario. Supply planning simulation is one of the major ways of obtaining improvement in the plan, because it can compare the live environment to a second environment, which usually has one factor changed.

This is a controlled experiment, where the live environment is the control, and the simulation environment is the test. This comparison can quickly provide insights into whether the change made in the controlled simulation environment is beneficial enough to also make in the live system. Without a good simulation capability (and most companies do not presently have good simulation capabilities) change must be made in the live system based upon an untested hypothesis, or based upon quantitative analysis where samples are taken from the system and results are analyzed off-line. While off-line analysis with spreadsheets can help in hypothesis generation, nothing can replace simulation using a copy of the live system to find out actual results from changes to the master data.

The Heart of Supply Chain Simulation

Simulation is primarily about connecting the same application logic and user interface to multiple data sets (schemas, flat files, etc.) that are slight variations of one another, and then analyzing the output. For instance, one schema may contain normal lead-times and be called "Current State." The next schema might be called "Lead-Time Test" and may have the lead-times decreased by twenty percent on specific lanes to see what happens to costs if the company were to move toward a faster method of transportation. The results are then documented and shared with the decision makers. Running these types of "what-if" scenarios is what simulation is all about. An unlimited number of things can be tested and customized for analysis for the company's needs. Without the ability to simulate, there is a significant limitation placed upon how much any company can improve its supply planning system.

Now that we have established what simulation is and its benefits, we can move into discussing simulation with MEIO software.

Why MEIO Applications are Generally Good at Simulation

Simulation can be performed with any supply planning method; however, optimization tends to be more frequently used in simulation than the other supply planning methods (MRP/DRP, heuristics or allocation). In fact, due to the complexity of most cost optimizers, I have recommended for some time now that external general optimization solvers be used to simulate cost optimizers in order to properly tune and explain their behavior. Having worked with all the major supply planning methods,

I can say that I would most prefer to perform simulation with MEIO applications. There are some straightforward reasons for this, which are listed below:

1. The emphasis MEIO vendors have placed on making simulation a focus of their applications. This breaks down into two major areas:
   a. The data tools and open approach, which allow for high data management efficiency as well as multiple ways for companies to adjust data and to make copies of MEIO models.
   b. The user interface design of many of the MEIO applications that allows for simulation results to be easily understood.
2. The precision of control inherent in MEIO applications.

How Supply Planning Applications are Enabled for Simulation from a Data Perspective

Some supply planning applications are inherently designed for simulation. However, the problem is that every supply planning vendor, regardless of the method their system employs for simulation, or their simulation capabilities, declares their application to be extremely good at simulation. Saying that any particular application has the ability to perform simulation is not the same as saying or demonstrating that it is easy to use and maintain. Ease of use and ease of maintenance are necessary preconditions of simulation software, because in a resource- and time-restricted environment, difficult or complicated tasks tend to go undone. Anyone who would take issue with this should consider how little simulation is actually used versus how frequently it could be used in supply chain planning departments. Several things are necessary in order to have an effective simulation environment. Look for the following points when the vendor says that their application is "great" at simulation:

1. The models within the application must be easy to copy and delete.

2. The parameters in the model must be easy to locate and easy to change.

3. The application should have controls, critical to the supply chain goals, available to the user so that the controls can be easily changed (e.g., service levels that can be changed).

4. The application's user interface must provide good visibility, so that planning outcomes can be easily observed.

I do a lot of work in the well-known supply planning application SAP Supply Network Planner (SNP), and as a point of comparison, I rate SNP poorly in all of the above criteria. SAP SNP can only come close to meeting the first criteria, but it is not as easy to do this in SAP SNP as in many other applications. In addition to being poorly designed for simulation, SAP has a significant disadvantage because it does not allow its database to be accessed by standard database tools. Instead, clients must use SAP's antiquated transactions such as MASSD (a mass maintenance transaction), making maintenance and adjustments more difficult. The application also provides poor visibility when compared with applications that allow for standard database management front ends, such as TOAD and Navicat.

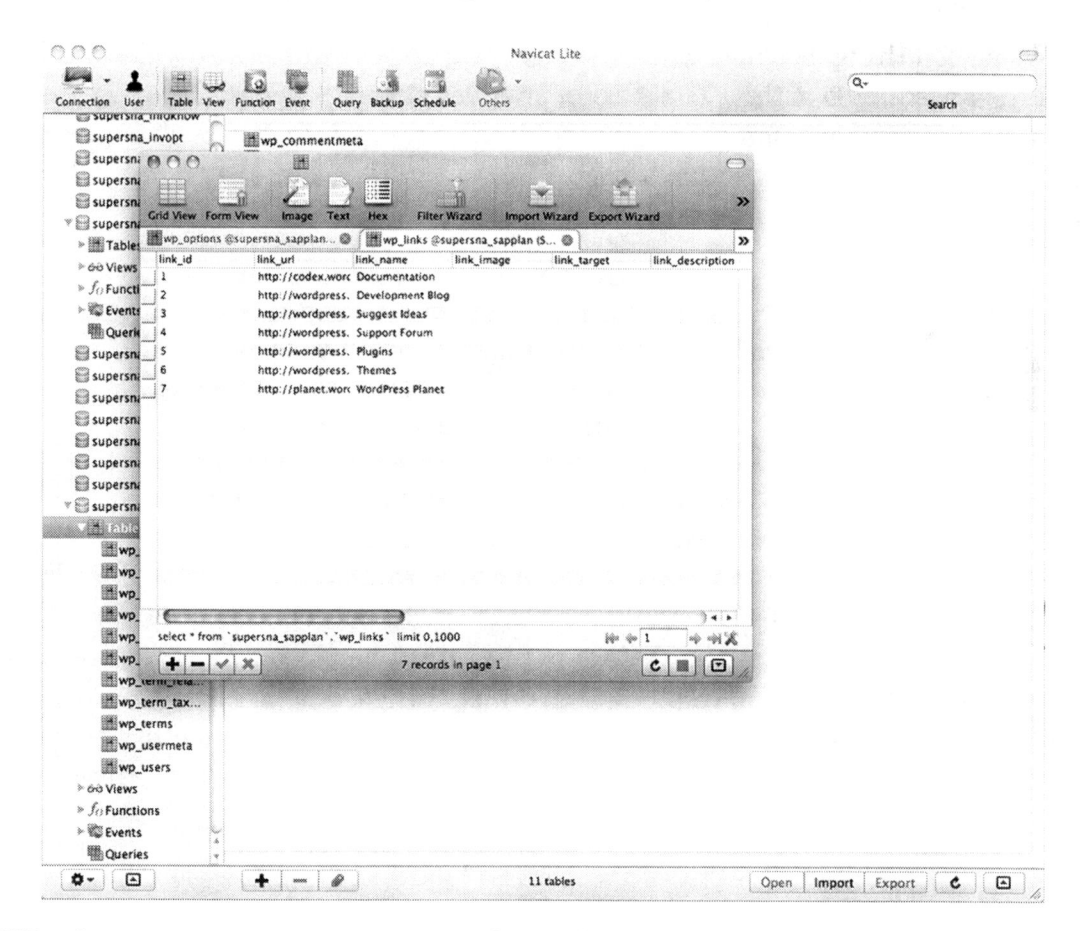

SQL schema management programs such as TOAD and Navicat allow people who are not necessarily DBAs to perform a number of SQL actions on a MEIO application database,

as well as to observe and export the data from an easy-to-understand interface. SQL Server by Microsoft also has a decent interface. Most MEIO vendors make accessing their schemas quite easy, showing the difference between them and SAP SNP as clearly as night and day.

Combining Segments of Different Schemas

The schemas of separate data (within the same database) are repositories for different saved models. Changing parameters easily is a feature of several MEIO vendors. None of them does anything one could not with a good understanding of SQL; however, they allow the changes to be more easily made by a wider group of people. This means that users require even less support from DBAs, which is always a good thing, because at most companies DBAs tend to be overloaded with work. As an example of this, ToolsGroup provides strong functionality in its ability to filter and sort parameters in order to make changes. In the ToolsGroup data view below, the parameters have been filtered by item, but they can be filtered by other model attributes as well, such as location.

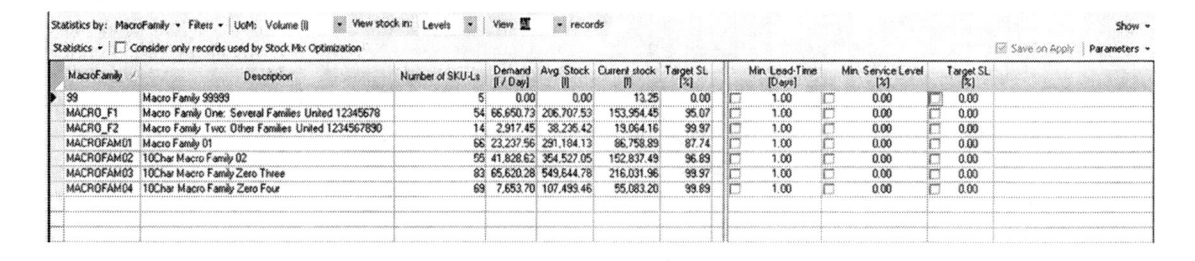

ToolsGroup allows for this precise filtering of parameters as well as for changing them, giving the user an additional way to change master data. Providing multiple pathways to alter the system is important because different people are more conformable with different ways of doing things. Applications that are less thoughtfully designed restrict the user to just one way of doing something, requiring each user to adjust to the application, rather than the other way around.

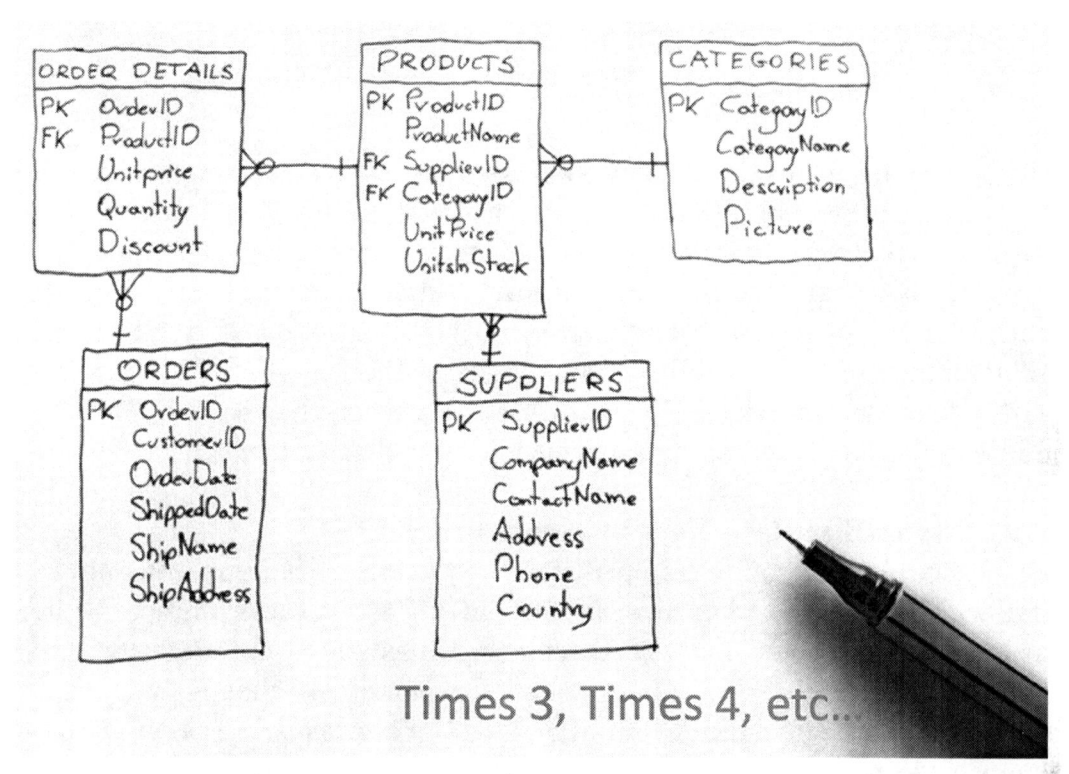

[Diagram: Database schema showing ORDER DETAILS, PRODUCTS, CATEGORIES, ORDERS, and SUPPLIERS tables with their relationships]

Times 3, Times 4, etc...

In addition to being able to connect a SQL front end to MEIO databases, many MEIO vendors have an even easier way to make changes to the underlying data. ToolsGroup, for example, has taken this a step further by providing the ability to copy different segments of existing schemas into an entirely new schema.

The Importance of Precision of Control in Simulation

The precision of control over the supply network is greatly improved with MEIO software versus other supply planning methods covered up to this point. Depending on the vendor, MEIO software also provides control of supply network inventory through the setting of service levels at different areas in the service level hierarchy as listed below:

- Location
- Product/location
- Customer

- Product mix
- Contract/equipment.

While service levels are most often discussed as control mechanisms, inventory levels can also control MEIO software. In this way the objective function becomes "minimize inventory investment" and the defined service levels become the constraints, rather than the other way around. There is no other supply planning method that allows such a precise change in the stocking position driven by such a small change in the controlling parameters of the software. This can become apparent to those experienced in supply planning when they see a MEIO application in simulation presented by an experienced application engineer.

The Ability to Simulate New Business and S&OP

Most supply planning simulation is designed to support improvements in the model, which in turn can improve operational efficiency. However, not all simulations have this goal. For instance, some companies distribute products for other companies or offer service level agreements to customers that include a cost for maintaining a supply chain. Simulations can be performed in order to forecast how much adding on new business to an existing supply network would cost. This is an important analysis because new business must be considered within the context of the inventory and product mix already carried in the existing supply network. MEIO software can then be used not only by supply planning but also by sales and groups responsible for generating the pricing on prospective contracts. This is one of the best opportunities for using MEIO applications and is covered in detail in Chapter 8: "MEIO and Service Level Agreements."

Another important function of simulation is to provide data to the sales and operations planning (S&OP) process. The majority of heavy lifting in S&OP calculations is not performed by S&OP software, but by the planning systems. The S&OP process will typically want multiple scenarios in order to plan for different circumstances, and this is something that MEIO software is well positioned to provide. To read more about how MEIO supports S&OP, see the post below:

http://www.scmfocus.com/inventoryoptimizationmultiechelon/2011/10/using-meio-to-connect-sales-and-supply-chain-planning/

Interface Aspects that Support Simulation

After the work to create a new simulation model has been performed on the data side, the changes must be visible to quickly and clearly see the outcomes. Changes can be made to master data, such as lead-times or minimum order quantities, or to the major business goals, such as inventory and service level. Servigistics *(formerly the MCA Solutions' application)* has a feature that allows for the inventory investment to be capped. In this instance, MEIO software will stop adding inventory to the plan when that cap is reached. When run this way, the inventory cap determines the service level rather than vice versa.

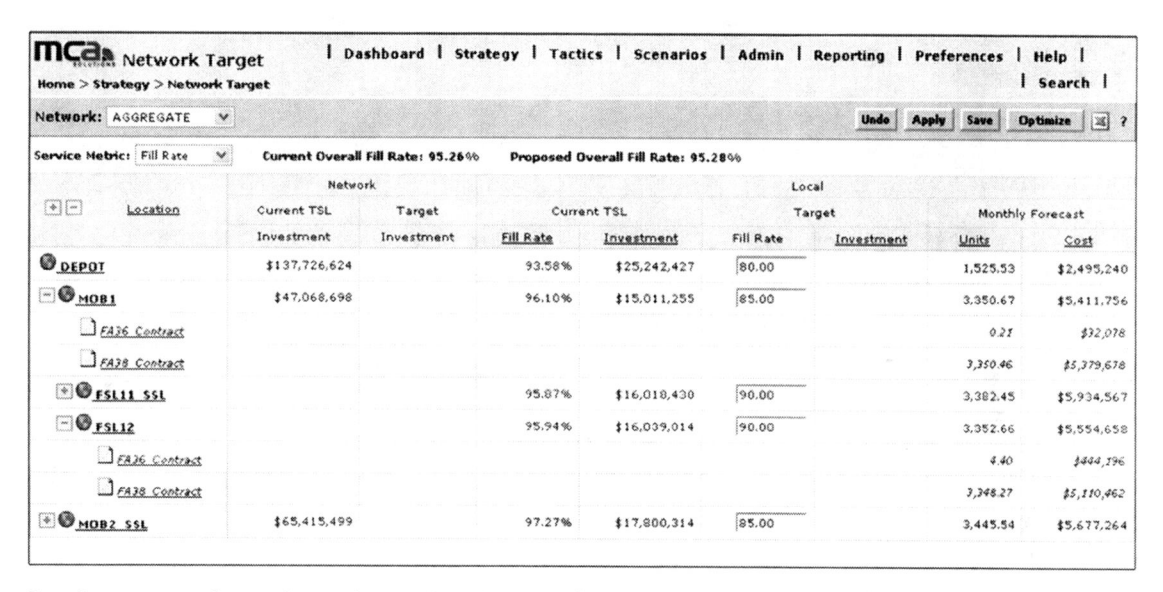

Location	Network Current TSL Investment	Target Investment	Current TSL Fill Rate	Investment	Local Target Fill Rate	Investment	Monthly Forecast Units	Cost
DEPOT	$137,726,624		93.58%	$25,242,427	80.00		1,525.53	$2,495,240
MOB1	$47,068,698		96.10%	$15,011,255	85.00		3,350.67	$5,411,756
FA36 Contract							0.21	$32,078
FA38 Contract							3,350.46	$5,379,678
FSL11 SSL			95.87%	$16,018,430	90.00		3,382.45	$5,934,567
FSL12			95.94%	$16,039,014	90.00		3,352.66	$5,554,658
FA36 Contract							4.40	$444,196
FA38 Contract							3,348.27	$5,110,462
MOB2 SSL	$65,415,499		97.27%	$17,800,314	85.00		3,445.54	$5,677,264

In the screenshot above from Servigistics' (formerly the MCA Solutions' application) Network Target screen, the model can be made to stop adding inventory after either reaching a service level target or a maximum inventory amount. The fill rate can be set for the overall network, for a location, or for a product location.

Logility provides a geographic-type view of the supply network with key measurements to the left and multiple application buttons with full descriptions in a bar along the top. Several drop-down menus change what is shown in the interface. As with Servigistics, this provides a global view on the supply network; however, notice that it approaches the interface from a completely different perspective.

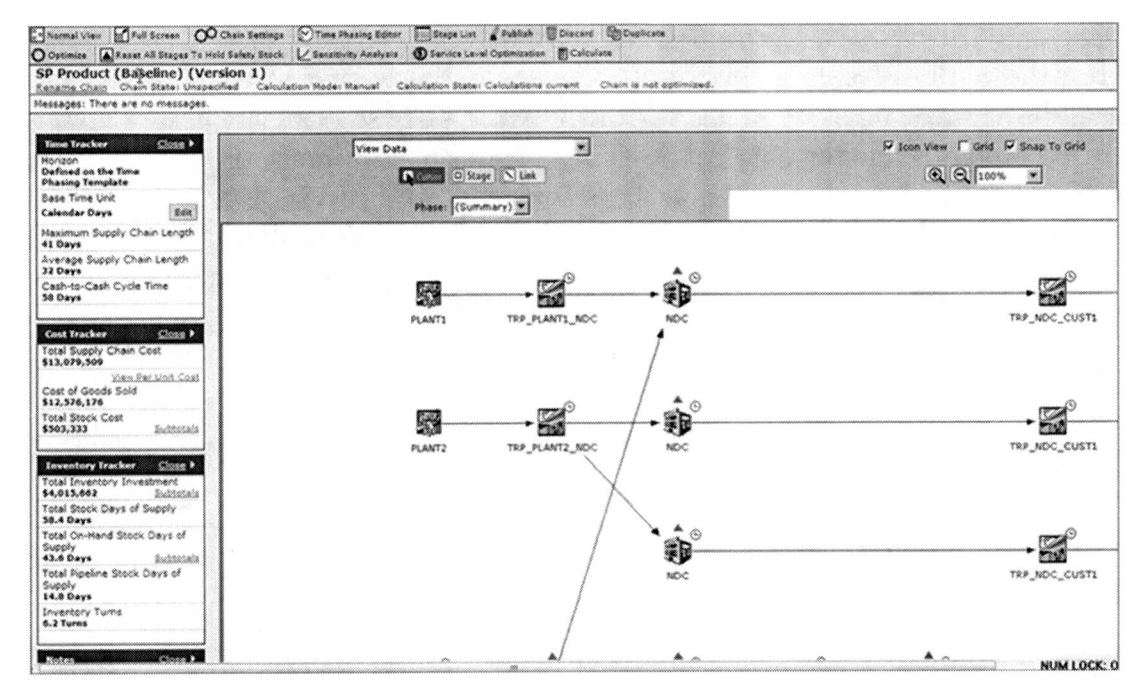

Logility Inventory Strategy Optimization has an overall network view that shows critical values to the left in addition to having the overall network listed to the right.

In my experience, MEIO vendors tend to offer better visibility to changes than non-MEIO vendors. I have not developed a hypothesis for why this tends to be the case, but it may be because many of the MEIO applications have been developed relatively recently. For whatever reason, MEIO vendors seem to encourage everyone to use their applications for strong visibility, a topic discussed in Appendix A: "MEIO Visibility and Analytics." Another example of visibility is provided by the ToolsGroup Network Browser view.

MEIO and Simulation 109

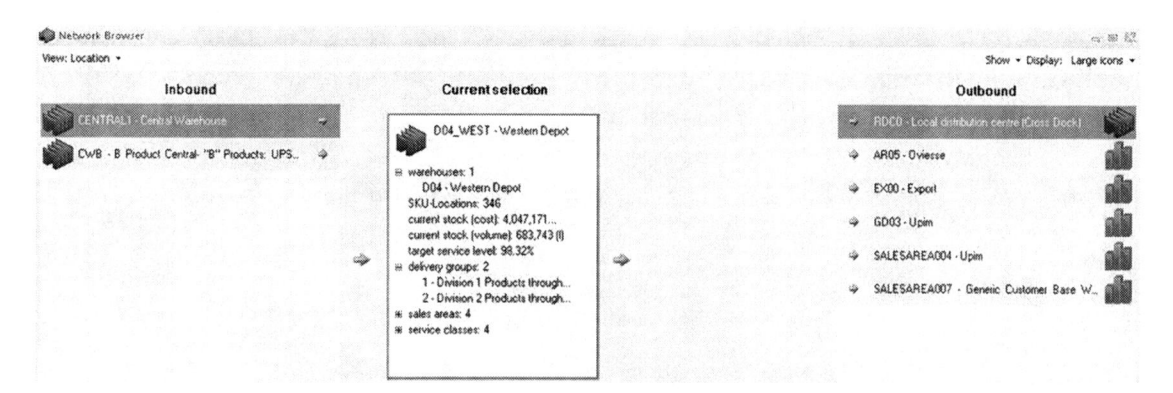

ToolsGroup's location view is an example of the high degree of visibility that can be brought to a supply planning application and to the supply network. One look at the ToolsGroup Network Browser shows which locations send material to this location and which locations receive material from this location, as well as a series of statistics related to the location. The information included on this screen is the following: the network level, SKU locations, current stock, target service level, delivery groups, sales areas, and service classes.

If either the inbound or the outbound location is selected, then the application moves that location to the center of the view with a corresponding change to the locations on either side of the center location. This is beneficial for three reasons:

1. This allows a quick cycling between views and the observation of many different statistics for each location.

2. It allows the planner to learn the location-to-location relationships in the supply network very quickly.

3. It allows a user to quickly gain an understanding of the valid location-to-location and location-material combinations.

Service Level and Inventory Investment Settings

Whenever I want to explain how inventory and service levels interact in a MEIO system, I like to show Servigistic's Network Proposed view. This screenshot shows a supply network to the left with both current and proposed (current and proposed are the results of two separate runs) service levels versus the respective inventory investments. This serves as both a control screen and reporting screen, allowing these values (either service levels or inventory investment per planning run) to be set globally, or at each location, or at the contract/equipment level. If users want to change a setting, they can change any single input variable, rerun the plan, and receive the new result all in one screen.

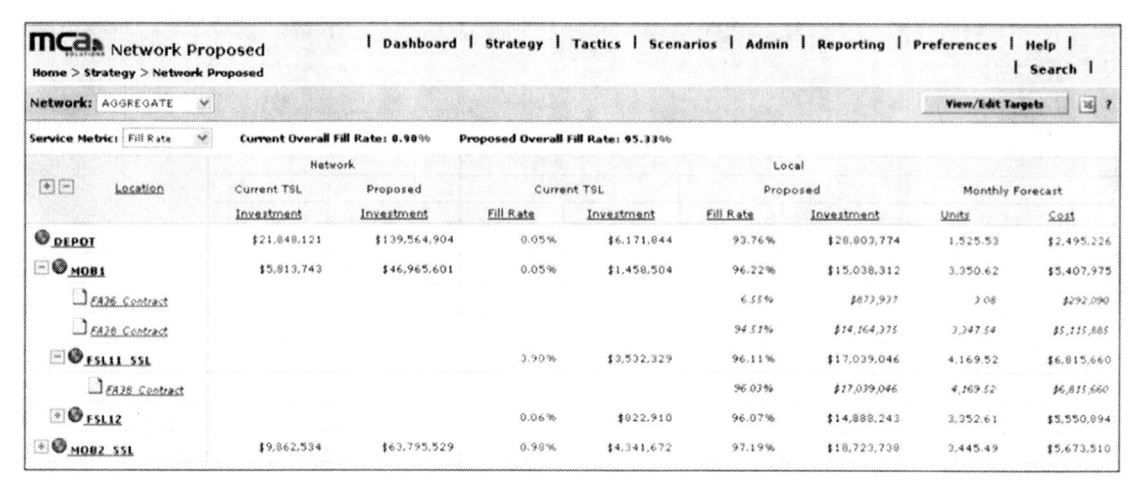

This function allows the planner to run a simulation and check the results, but not overwrite the previous run, making it faster and easier to see how much the new simulation changed due to target changes. This is an example of an application that was designed from its initial stages with simulation in mind.

Accuracy of Simulation Provided by MEIO Applications

The best MEIO vendors model from "the bottom up." So far in this chapter we have reviewed several easy-to-understand screens from MEIO vendors that display high-level numbers such as service levels versus inventory investment. However, these high-level analytical screens are the emergent result of many thousands of individual stocking decisions. After running a MEIO simulation, high-level views can be interpreted and individual item locations can be viewed to see what stocking positions have been changed between runs. The planners can then drill into the detail very quickly to see if they agree with the planning result for their individual product.

This also means that no shortcuts are taken to arrive at the simulation results. Short cuts are a common limitation with many supply chain strategy projects that apply overly-simplified modeling mathematics that are unable to create sufficiently accurate predictions of what will happen if changes to the supply network are made. Richard Wallis, of ToolsGroup, explains the point quite convincingly that once ToolsGroup is used to model a client supply chain strategically, the client then has a system that is ready to be moved into production. My interview with Richard on this topic can be seen at the link below and I think it is very worthwhile for anyone with an interest in this topic.

http://www.vimeo.com/15060562

Initial Versus Post Go-Live Simulation
Simulation is important for the development of the initial configuration settings, and for post go-live use. Simulation allows for the periodic adjustment of the model parameters to either improve the planning outcome or to adjust to changing conditions in the business environment. The ease of use of the simulation environment is critical, because the faster and more easily simulation can be performed, the more simulations on different factors can be completed, the higher the value to the business, and the better and more quickly the supply plan can be made to approach its potential. Easy-to-use systems that naturally encourage the performance of simulation create a positive feedback loop for the companies intelligent enough to set their systems up in this way.

Strategic Versus Online Simulations
Increasingly, I find that the best applications build simulation capability into the same window as the production view. This is different from applications that follow the older method, which compelled the user to go into different instances. This new approach allows for more efficient and ad hoc simulation, which in turn allows the user to perform simulation very quickly and as part of their normal planning process. If the user likes the simulation results better than the initial results, the user can eliminate the initial run and keep the simulation version. In fact, when software is set up in this manner, the present planning run is simply another simulation. A vendor that does this very well is PlanetTogether. They make production scheduling software rather than supply planning software, but their implementation of simulation is so well designed that I am showcasing it here to demonstrate this concept.

In the PlanetTogether application, a new tab designates a simulation version. In this way, the initial version is simply another version at the planner's disposal. The planner has the option of keeping or deleting either the active tab or the simulation tab. If the active tab is deleted, the simulation tab and all of its corresponding data becomes the active version. There is no limit to how many times the planner can make adjustments, test outputs and delete simulation or active tabs and versions.

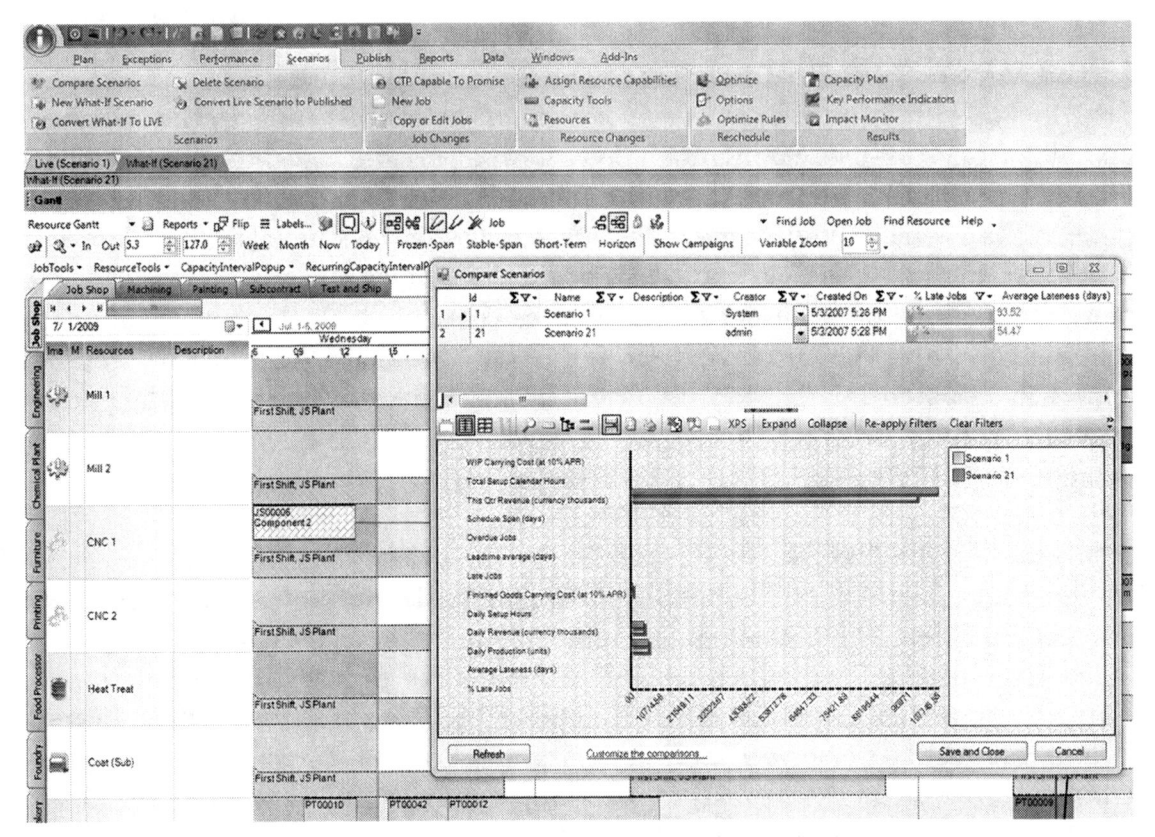

PlanetTogether offers a best-practice for how to manage simulation scenarios. Very little complexity is placed upon the planner in order to run simulation. The simulation is seamlessly integrated into the normal planning process, which should be the ultimate goal of simulation software development. The more effortless the simulation and the more integrated it is into the normal production version, the more effective it becomes, and the more commonly it will be used.

Finally, no plan is solidified, or sent to the ERP system, until the planner signs off on the best simulation version. The planner then keeps the "winning" parameters and uses them for subsequent planning runs.

Conclusion

Supply planning simulation is a method of making controlled changes in duplicate data models in order to analyze how the output changes as a result. MEIO vendors seem to understand the power of simulation and have built strong simulation capabilities into their products. Three major reasons that explain why MEIO is so good at simulation are: the flexible data capabilities that are available; a number of MEIO application user interfaces that are strong in visibility; and of course, the precision of control inherent in MEIO applications. While traditionally used to improve the settings of the planning system, simulation can also be used to price new business (for those companies that offer direct supply chain management services to other companies, or for those that service items for other companies). Simulation is also used to support the S&OP process.

Some MEIO vendors offer simulation comparisons within the same window as the production system view. Simulation by itself can be used to justify the acquisition of MEIO software—and, in fact, a number of MEIO vendors offer desktop versions of their solution. These provide all of the simulation capabilities of the enterprise versions used in production, but at a greatly reduced cost. Because supply planning simulation in general has so many opportunities for improvement, it will be interesting to see if companies use all the simulation capabilities built into MEIO applications.

Supply chain simulation is a detailed subject that can be analyzed from numerous angles, and this chapter was designed to provide specifics for simulation as it applies to MEIO applications. Supply planning simulation is greatly underutilized for a number of reasons, not the least of which is the limited ease of use of simulation in several very popular supply planning systems. However, a lack of knowledge of how simulation should be run, managed and documented is another factor. I maintain a sub-blog that focuses on supply chain simulation in more general terms, which can be accessed at the link below:

   http://www.scmfocus.com/supplychainsimulation/

CHAPTER 8

MEIO and Service Level Agreements

Background

One of the more interesting uses for MEIO is supporting service level agreements (SLAs). SLAs are methods of charging different customers different prices for different levels of service. The article "Winning in the Aftermarket" in the *Harvard Business Review* explains SLAs well:

> Companies must design a portfolio of service products; different customers have different service needs even though they may own the same product. For example, when a mainframe computer in a stock exchange fails, the financial impact will be more severe than when a mainframe in a library goes down.

SLAs began in the service market, but are moving into the finished goods market, as many companies increasingly want to manage their supply chains and customers by differentiated service levels. This is a very common goal for many finished goods manufacturers and distributors. In my estimation, most are still unaware that MEIO is the key technology for enabling SLAs. It is still far more common for the group that prices and negotiates SLA contracts to use completely different applications (often home-grown spreadsheets) from the group that plans and manages the supply chain. This presents a big opportunity to integrate two functions much more tightly.

SLAs have been in existence for quite some time and are very well understood as a method of managing a business. Yet while MEIO is over a decade old, it is still new to many, and so it is easy to determine that the vast majority of SLAs are not supported by any MEIO application. Combining the terms "SLA" and "inventory optimization" and "service level agreement" and "inventory optimization" in web searches produces some commercially motivated material, but not much detailed information about the relationship aside from my own articles at SCM Focus (and this is really only evidence that I personally find the topic of interest, which is not what I am checking for). In terms of books, the most coverage I have found is in *Analysis and Algorithms for Service Parts Supply Chains,* by J. A. Muckstadt. In this book, the author discusses the mathematics necessary to support various service agreements. However, I have not found information for general consumption in any book, despite the fact that the concept and relationship between SLAs and MEIO is very well known by all of the service parts planning vendors. The two concepts are very much made for each other. I hope this book is used to provide a general understanding of the connection between SLAs and MEIO.

The History of SLAs

SLAs developed as a method for guaranteeing a certain level of service for a specific level of compensation. The SLA provider is required to meet the stipulations in the contract or is required to compensate the SLA customer.

SLAs have become common in all types of businesses, from telecom to aerospace and defense. SLAs are similar to software as a solution (SaaS) in that they closely tie the incentives of the customer and the provider. I once interviewed Erik Larkin at Arena Solutions, and he discussed how good things happen when the incentives of companies and customers are in alignment. When I was interviewing Erik and listening to his comments on SaaS, I immediately thought of SLAs. Although Erik Larkin and Nathan Martin are speaking of SaaS solutions in the following video, the same could be said for SLAs.

http://www.scmfocus.com/supplychaininnovation/2010/10/eric-larkin-and-nathan-martin-from-arena-solutions-on-the-benefits-of-saas/

One of the best-known and most effective users of SLAs is the networking giant Cisco. You can read about their SLA program at their website:

http://www.cisco.com/en/US/products/ps6602/products_ios_protocol_group_home.html

While Cisco's products can be a bit obscure for those who do not work in networking, just about everyone is familiar with Google Apps. Google Apps offers both a free and paid version, and under the paid version, they offer an SLA, which you can read about below or see at their website:

Google Apps

Businesses	**Google Apps Service Level Agreement**
Schools	Google Apps SLA. During the Term of the applicable Google Apps Agreement (the "Agreement"), the Google Apps
Organizations	Covered Services web interface will be operational and available to Customer at least 99.9% of the time in any calendar month (the "Google Apps SLA"). If Google does not meet the Google Apps SLA, and if Customer meets its obligations under this Google Apps SLA, Customer will be eligible to receive the Service Credits described
Applications	below. This Google Apps SLA states Customer's sole and exclusive remedy for any failure by Google to meet the
Admin features	Google Apps SLA.
Tours & demos	Definitions. The following definitions shall apply to the Google Apps SLA.
Customers	"Downtime" means, for a domain, if there is more than a five percent user error rate. Downtime is measured
Apps Marketplace	based on server side error rate.
FAQ	"Google Apps Covered Services" means the Gmail, Google Calendar, Google Talk, Google Docs, Google Groups and Google Sites components of the Service. This does not include the Gmail Labs functionality, Google Apps – Postini Services, Gmail Voice or Video Chat components of the Service.
News & events	
Contact sales	"Monthly Uptime Percentage" means total number of minutes in a calendar month minus the number of minutes of Downtime suffered in a calendar month, divided by the total number of minutes in a calendar
Support	month.
	"Service" means the Google Apps for Business service (also known as Google Apps Premier Edition), Google Apps for Government service, Google Apps for ISPs service (also known as Google Apps Partner Edition), or Google Apps for Education service (also known as Google Apps Education Edition) (as applicable) provided by Google to Customer under the Agreement.

http://www.google.com/apps/intl/en/terms/sla.html

Standard Limitations in Supply Network Control

Supply chain departments at companies are continually challenged by service level control, for two main reasons:

1. They lack the correct software to control service level the way they want.

2. They often cannot agree upon the service levels (beyond very high level goals).

It is strangely inconsistent that so many companies have so much focus on service levels, but lack the software to control service levels.

Most supply planning methods lack the mechanism to control service levels the way that companies would like, requiring companies to spend an extraordinary amount of time managing service levels. These companies have service level controls, but most of these controls, such as the days' supply (as described in Chapter 4: "Multi-Echelon Planning Explained"), are indirect. Dynamic safety stock can only be set at the product-location combination. Service level is a critical key performance indicator (KPI) to which the bonuses of higher-ups are tied, but which can only be controlled indirectly. Without the proper control mechanism, supply chain planning becomes more reactive and execution oriented. This is a problem at many companies.

To understand this, it's important to review how the goals of supply chain organizations are set. Directors at supply chain organizations are given different service level objectives by their vice presidents. VPs receive pressure on service level attainment from their sales organizations. The VP must keep inventories down, but must simultaneously satisfy the sales side by keeping the service levels high. Often salespeople will contact the supply chain director(s) and ask that a particular customer be given priority over others. These interactions may result in emails to directors needing them to "understand" how important this or that customer is to the business. The director then writes emails back stating that the sales organizations must "understand" that the supply chain organization faces certain constraints. However, as much as sales or the supply chain department proposes a service level for a product location (or for a customer's product), there is no clear evidence that the customer is willing to pay for the service level requested. This means that some customers may be paying a higher price than they want to and thus are more likely to go to a competitor; this also means that some customers are paying too low of a price, depressing the profits of the company that is managing the supply chain in question. This is where SLAs come in to play.

SLAs and MEIO

SLAs serve as the organizing concept and the contract, while MEIO performs the heavy lifting that helps companies quantify how they should price the SLA.

The concept of SLAs allows for the most direct expression of the customer's will (and ability to pay) as applied across the company's supply chain. MEIO is the enabling technology that allows the SLA to express itself in what results in SKU holding positions and locations.

Focus On Service Level Agreements

Service Level Agreement Configuration

This document from Sun Microsystems describes how SLAs should be created for a data center:

http://www.sun.com/blueprints/0402/sla.pdf

The above document describes how a good SLA addresses five key areas:

1. What the provider is promising
2. How the provider will deliver on those promises
3. Who will measure delivery and how
4. What happens if the provider fails to deliver as promised
5. How the SLA will change over time

The document goes on to explain the importance of basing the SLA on operational realities. The challenge for a new service and its associated SLA is that there is a direct relationship between the operational environment and the maximum levels of availability that can be promised. Thus, an SLA cannot be created in a vacuum. An SLA must be defined with the infrastructure in mind. A nonlinear relationship exists between the levels of availability and related costs. Some customers need higher levels of availability and are willing to pay more; therefore, having different SLAs with different associated costs is a common approach.

Reducing Friction between the Sales Organization and Supply Chain

The constant friction between sales and operations described in the previous paragraphs is due in large to the fact that the incentives of sales organizations and supply chain organizations are not aligned. This is true both in overall terms and among the smaller units within the organizations. Much of the effort and conflict comes from determining which customers will receive priority over others. For example, salespeople benefit more if their customers receive more inventory and a higher service level than the company's direct customers. When incentives are misaligned (and in truth sales and operations tend to be misaligned regardless of the company or industry), it becomes more critical to have the necessary information to quantify the key decision-making variables in order to resolve the conflict. Without a strong connection between sales and supply chain/operations, salespeople can propose that some customers are more important than others (this customer is bigger, older, or more profitable and thus deserves priority). This is a prescription for conflict and shifting objectives, as competing interests become more or less influential over time. Thus, what often happens is that the biggest customer takes precedence. This is not necessarily the best decision for the company, however, as smaller companies may be more profitable. Some companies draw no distinctions between customers, and attempt—at least on paper—to satisfy all customers at the same service level. Indeed this may work for some companies, but other companies that could benefit from offering different service levels to different customers don't do this because they lack the tools and capabilities to do so. SLAs can certainly help in this area.

MEIO for SLA Pricing

MEIO can also be used to allow the sales side of businesses to effectively price SLAs by understanding the actual costs to serve customers. It costs less to add new business and new product volumes to a pre-existing supply network than to add business to a completely new supply network. The more volume a supply network manages, the lower the average cost is per unit or per customer. While new customers sometimes ask the company to stock new products, generally, when a potential customer approaches a company for a quotation, the majority of items will already be stocked. This is called "incremental pricing," and MEIO software can perform this incremental pricing with a high degree of accuracy.

MEIO and Service Level Agreements 121

This is important because obviously the vast majority of quotations are provided to customers who will simply add volume to an existing supply network. Below is a graphic that describes incremental pricing.

Supply Network
Incremental Pricing

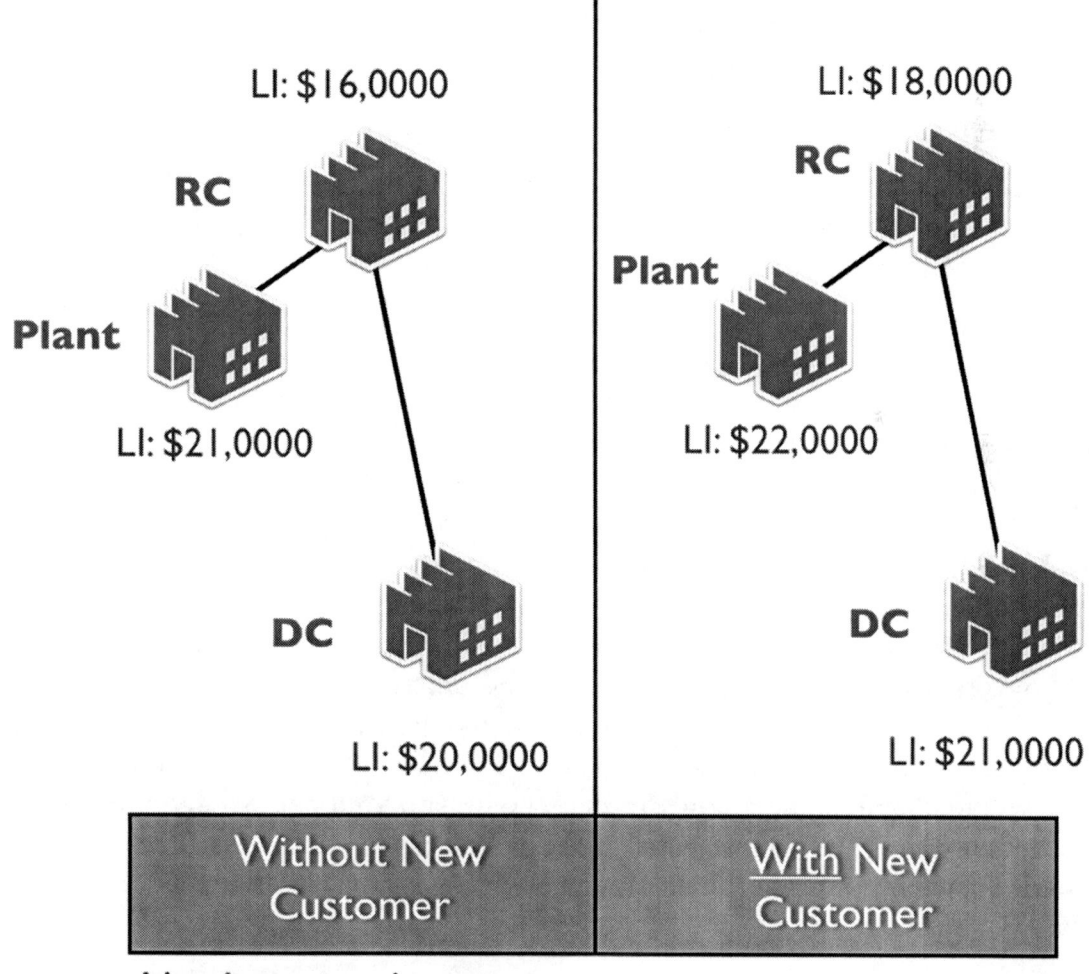

Without New Customer
- RC — LI: $16,0000
- Plant — LI: $21,0000
- DC — LI: $20,0000

With New Customer
- RC — LI: $18,0000
- Plant — LI: $22,0000
- DC — LI: $21,0000

LI = Location Inventory
Incremental inventory cost is **$4000**

How the Shared Sales/Supply Chain MEIO Instance Works

The sales department does not have to configure or populate the MEIO application with master data. Most of this work has already been done by the supply planning department as part the preparation required for using the application to run the business. All the sales department needs to do is the following:

1. Log-in to a simulation version of the application to add any new products that are necessary to be carried in order to acquire the potential customer.

2. Add the projected new sales volumes for the potential customer.

3. Run the model to simulate various customer service level targets that will result in new and higher total inventory costs.

4. Subtract the inventory costs generated by the simulation from the inventory costs in the production system to arrive at the net increase in inventory caused by the addition of the potential customer's volume.

5. Document the results so that they can be used for the response to the customer, as well as for archival purposes.

The inventory figure calculated by the MEIO application is used as a base. Storage costs, transportation costs and other overhead can be added to the base inventory figure by way of separate calculations or by way of proportional factors. Once developed, these factors can be reused with some slight adjustment for future pricing efforts. Finally, a margin percentage is added to arrive at a final price to present to the prospective SLA customer. This margin can fluctuate based upon market conditions and other factors the sales department may want to include; however, the costs on which the margins are applied should be consistent in their calculation for all assessments of this type. That is, if the sales department very much wants a deal, it should only reduce the margin and not fool itself by adjusting the costs to make the projected margin look better than it is. The following graphic shows a sample scenario of new business cost estimation.

Service Level Control Issues

- Service Levels Determined Internally, and Loosely Connected to Customer Needs
- Lack of Ability to Directly Control the Supply Plan With Service Level

There are a number of benefits to this model, which features a high degree of information sharing. The sales organization and supply chain organization become customers of one another, each providing different information to the process and each sharing the use of the MEIO application. The end result is the capability to produce a far more accurate price that is based upon a comprehensive appraisal of the company's costs to deliver the service level requested. In addition, the costs of the MEIO solution are shared across more areas of the business, making the implementation of software more cost effective, with the added benefit of more effectively tying together sales and operations.

Service Level Contracting and Planning

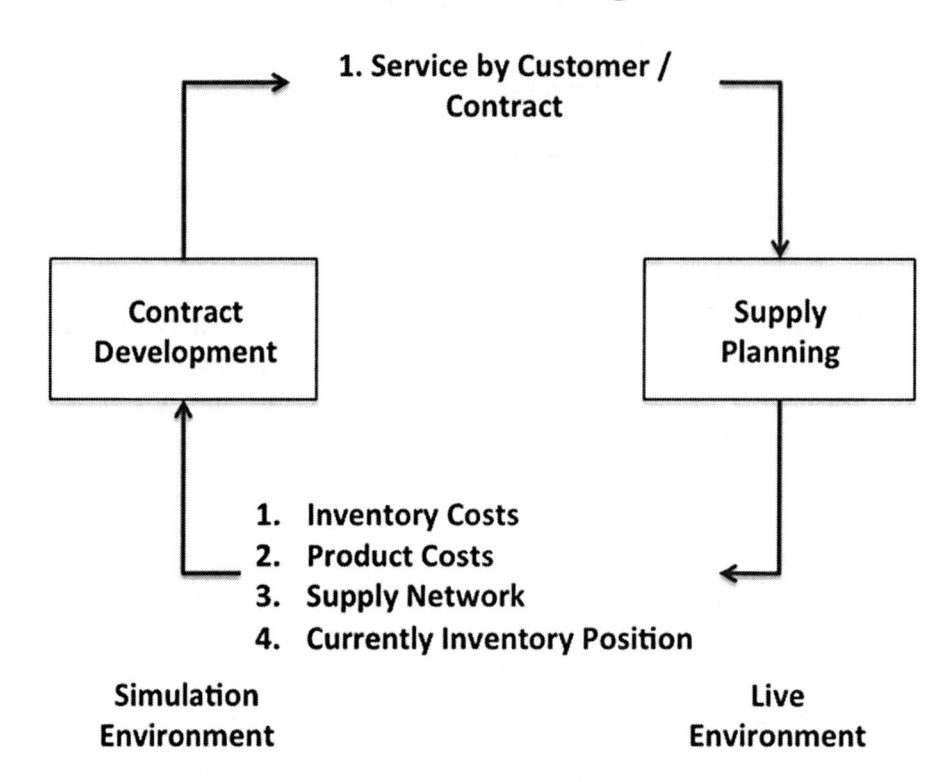

```
                    1. Service by Customer /
                          Contract
        ┌─────────────────→                ─────────────────┐
        │                                                    ↓
┌──────────────┐                                    ┌──────────────┐
│   Contract   │                                    │    Supply    │
│ Development  │                                    │   Planning   │
└──────────────┘                                    └──────────────┘
        ↑                                                    │
        │        1. Inventory Costs                          │
        │        2. Product Costs                            │
        └────────3. Supply Network ──────────────────────────┘
                 4. Currently Inventory Position

    Simulation                                            Live
    Environment                                        Environment
```

SLAs do not solve every problem, but they do a good job of quantitatively setting a company's customer priorities. MEIO software, which can set contract service levels, can plan for a list of customers who purchase their products like the one below.

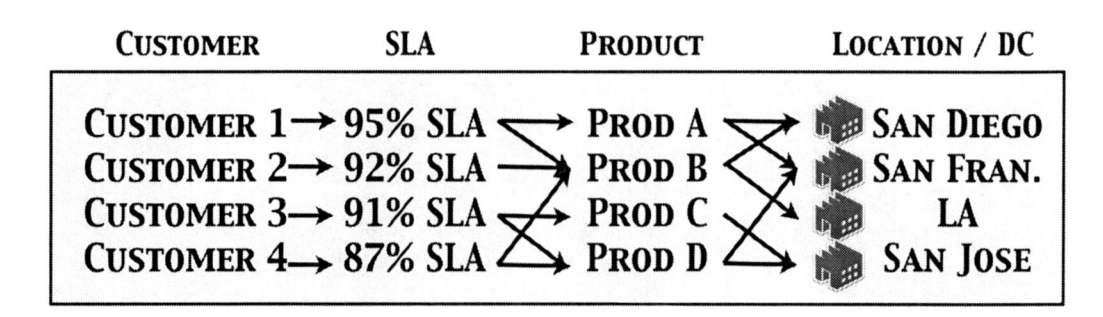

CUSTOMER	SLA	PRODUCT	LOCATION / DC
CUSTOMER 1	95% SLA	PROD A	SAN DIEGO
CUSTOMER 2	92% SLA	PROD B	SAN FRAN.
CUSTOMER 3	91% SLA	PROD C	LA
CUSTOMER 4	87% SLA	PROD D	SAN JOSE

Providing a Menu of Options to Customers

The combination of SLAs and MEIO is very empowering to the company that has the ability to accurately price new business as this new business can be sustainably supported by the company's supply chain. MEIO allows companies to provide a "menu of options" to customers like the one listed below.

Service Level	SLA Cost
95%	= $2,854,000
92%	= $2,290,000
87%	= $1,830,000
85%	= $1,512,000

A company with this type of capability can ask their prospective customer how much they would be willing to pay. Based on this information, the company can then provide the prospective customer with an estimated service level. Alternatively, the company can publish a list of service levels and costs from which the customer can choose a service level that fits their needs.

Conclusion

What began in the service market has proven to be applicable to the finished goods market as well. SLAs have the benefit of tying the sales and operations departments together, and MEIO is a main enabling technology for SLAs. There is a very significant opportunity for MEIO applications to add value to the sales process at many companies because MEIO has the ability to improve not only the internal planning of the supply chain, but also to assist companies in pricing new business. When SLAs are supported by MEIO, the company's incentives can be aligned with those of their customers. SLAs can be supported by the information provided from MEIO applications, which do the heavy lifting to quantify the actual costs for the provision of services at different service levels. MEIO applications do not quantify every cost associated with an SLA. Instead, they calculate the inventory costs of meeting different service objectives. They do not calculate the transportation costs, labor costs, or other costs that make up the total cost of the SLA. Instead, they provide an accurate base from which to apply proportional factors that represent those costs. MEIO applications can also provide inventory costs and results for different levels of service, from low to very high service levels. This approach is new to so many companies and in order to move to this model, companies will have to make significant adjustment. Implementing this shared solution effectively will require a new way for sales and operations to work together and to share information as well as the MEIO application.

CHAPTER 9

How MEIO is Different from APS and MRP/DRP

Background

Chapter 6: "MEIO Versus Cost Optimization" covered how these two related supply planning methods compared to one another. This chapter is also comparative, but broadens this analysis to include how MEIO differs from all the supply planning methods.

As is described in Chapters 2, 4, 6 and 8, MEIO is fundamentally different from MRP/DRP and APS systems in the way in which it approaches the problem of supply planning. Part of this relates to the objective function (or goal) of the optimization, which in the case of MEIO is the maximization of service level minimization of inventory investment. Another important difference is that MEIO has the ability to calculate stocking a position at one location by relating it to the stocking position at a different location connected to it in the supply network (the multi-echelon component). A third difference is that MEIO more closely approximates the objectives that companies have with regard to their supply chains.

Different Assumptions

MEIO makes different assumptions than the other supply planning methods. Two important differences are listed below.

1. The Location Independent Assumption
2. The Sequential Processing of the Supply Network

When implementing a MEIO solution, it's important to socialize how these assumptions are different and why they make the output different (and actually better) to what both the planners and decision makers are accustomed to using.

The Location Independent Assumption

MRP/DRP and all the APS supply planning methods are similar in that they share a *less accurate* assumption: location independence. All of the supply planning methods prior to MEIO plans the locations in the supply network as "islands," as if the stocking at one location does not affect the stocking level at another location. The multi-echelon portion of MEIO takes a more sophisticated approach, and has the mathematics to model interdependence that non-multi-echelon systems do not. The mathematics for supporting multi-echelon functionality is complex, and it took quite some time for it to move from the research phase to implementation. Although research into these topics can be traced back to as early as 1958, the software to implement this research was not introduced until the late 1990s. This can be seen in the timeline on the next page.

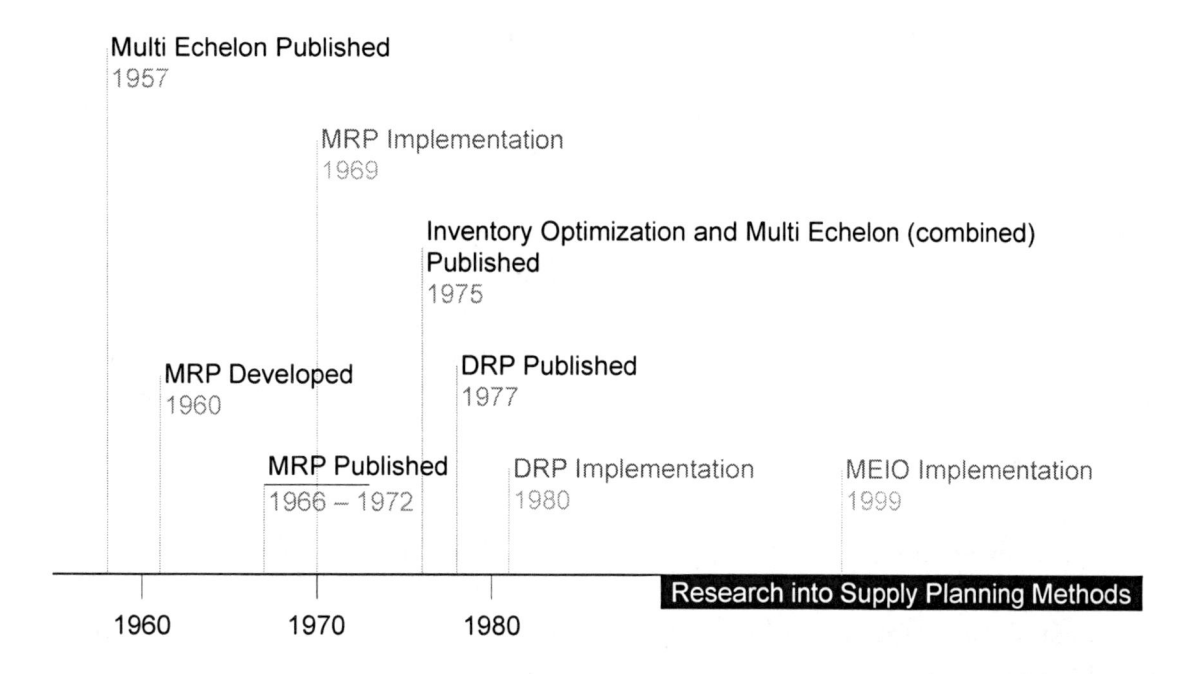

Research into Supply Planning Methods

- Multi Echelon Published — 1957
- MRP Developed — 1960
- MRP Published — 1966–1972
- MRP Implementation — 1969
- Inventory Optimization and Multi Echelon (combined) Published — 1975
- DRP Published — 1977
- DRP Implementation — 1980
- MEIO Implementation — 1999

Multi-echelon accurately accounts for the fact that the locations in the supply network are *interdependent* and that service levels and inventory are the main drivers of the supply plan. Effectively understanding and interpreting the output of MEIO means understanding how its assumptions are different from other supply planning systems. Joseph Shamir of ToolsGroup has some interesting things to say about how MEIO changes the assumptions that many supply chain professionals have held for some time.

http://www.vimeo.com/15101084

The Sequential Processing of the Supply Network

MRP/DRP and APS methods make a second assumption that limits their ability to position inventory with the same accuracy that is possible with MEIO applications, and this relates to the little-discussed topic of how the various methods process product-location combinations. These older methods perform a sequential process during their planning operations. MRP, DRP and heuristics look at one location-product combination at a time, until they have processed all the location-product combinations. Both DRP and heuristics can consider multiple receiving locations, and do things like distributing the inventory evenly between multiple receiving locations in situations where there is a shortage or overage of demand versus the available stock. (This is called fair share distribution) However, they are still processing the sending location one at a time.

Allocation is actually an order-based planning system that has a very different sequence of processing than MRP, DRP or heuristics. Allocation breaks up the problem into specific orders, and processes the supply network one order at a time. It is the only supply planning method that processes in this manner. When all demands have been processed (some accepted and some rejected based upon planned stock), the plan is complete.

Decomposition in Cost Optimization

The methods we have discussed up to this point (MRP/DRP, heuristics and allocation), all work relatively simply in terms of how they process the supply network. However, cost optimization becomes significantly more complex. Cost optimization breaks the supply network problem into a series of sub-problems that can be defined in the configuration. In optimization, the segmentation of a problem into smaller problems is called decomposition, which literally means to "decompose" the problem as described in Wikipedia:

> Decomposition in computer science, also known as factoring, refers to the process by which a complex problem or system is broken down into parts that are easier to conceive, understand, program, and maintain.

This topic is covered in more detail in this post:

http://www.scmfocus.com/sapplanning/2011/10/12/snp-optimizer-sub-problem-division-and-decomposition/

As an example, in the SAP SNP optimizer, three methods are available for decomposition:

1. Time
2. Product

3. Resource

The most common way of performing decomposition in supply planning cost optimizers is by product. Taking all locations that carry a single product and solving for that much smaller problem, rather than solving the much bigger problem of all products and locations, accomplishes this. This segmented sub-network is then called a "sub-problem." The overall problem of planning the supply network is broken into many different sub-network sub-problems. The cost optimizer operates in this manner because it does not look at the entire network at once, but segregates the supply network by product. The general intent of decomposition is to divide the overall problem into as many small problems as possible (in order to minimize processing effort), while not interfering with the relationships that span the sub-problems. The relationships must be respected to provide a good solve. This is why the selection of the right decomposition method requires an understanding of the business.

The following combination of product and locations may be one sub-problem.

Decomposition Example: Product ABC
Locations: San Diego, DC; San Francisco, RDC; Los Angeles, DC; San Jose, DC

Focus On Cost Optimization Run Duration

Unless the problem being solved is simple (and most supply network problems with full production volumes are not simple), optimizers are generally given windows of time within which they must come to a solution. The determination of what this window of time should be is based upon what is commonly called the operational workflow between systems—the time available for system processing and the sending and receiving of data between systems. This is necessary because optimization tends to run longer than the operational workflow will allow. Setting a cap for the processing time can often bring good solutions, and allowing the optimizer to continue to run after a certain point does not necessarily lead to significantly better solutions. However, in order to find this point, iterative testing at different durations must be performed. This is accomplished by running the optimizer for varying amounts of time and showing the results to planners to determine at what point the optimizer reaches the point of diminishing marginal utility, or the benefits of the results. If the runtime is too long to achieve the optimal business benefit, then changes can be made to the optimizer model, or extra hardware and things like parallel processing profiles can be set up (advisable regardless) to help reduce the optimizer runtime. Adding hardware is generally the least expensive option, and is becoming less expensive per power level every year. However, quite often configuration changes that could improve runtime are left unaddressed by the design and implementation phases.

How MEIO Differs in Terms of Sequential Processing

MEIO diverges quite radically from the non-sequential processing of the previous methods. This is the type of detail that tends to get overlooked; however, the way in which MEIO processes the supply network is the reason it can do some things that other supply planning methods cannot. Instead of being sequential, MEIO is the one supply planning method that does not process the supply network sequentially. The MEIO algorithm for processing the supply network roughly approximates the following (although details differ by vendor):

1. Calculate all possible stocking decisions for the entire supply network.

2. Select the one that makes the largest contribution to the system service level.

3. Recalculate the next stage of all possible stocking decisions and select the best one, and so on.

At every iteration multi-echelon functionality has compared all the product location combinations of the supply network, and of course all the echelons, hence the name "multi-echelon."

How MEIO Compares Graphically to the Other Supply Planning Methods

Understanding how the various supply planning methods compare to one another in practice is important. Supply chain professionals tend to become very experienced in the one method they work with. However, in many cases they do not have the opportunity to learn about the other methods until their company initiates a new project using that method. Once the distinctions between the methods are understood, mapping business requirements is a straightforward process. To this end, I have included several graphs that can help you understand how MEIO compares on several important criteria. These graphs are bound to be controversial, and they are not perfect "mathematical representations" of the truth. Actually, nothing could be because there is a natural subjectivity based upon the implementation experiences of the graph creator. They are, however, approximations based upon my own experience with all of these methods.

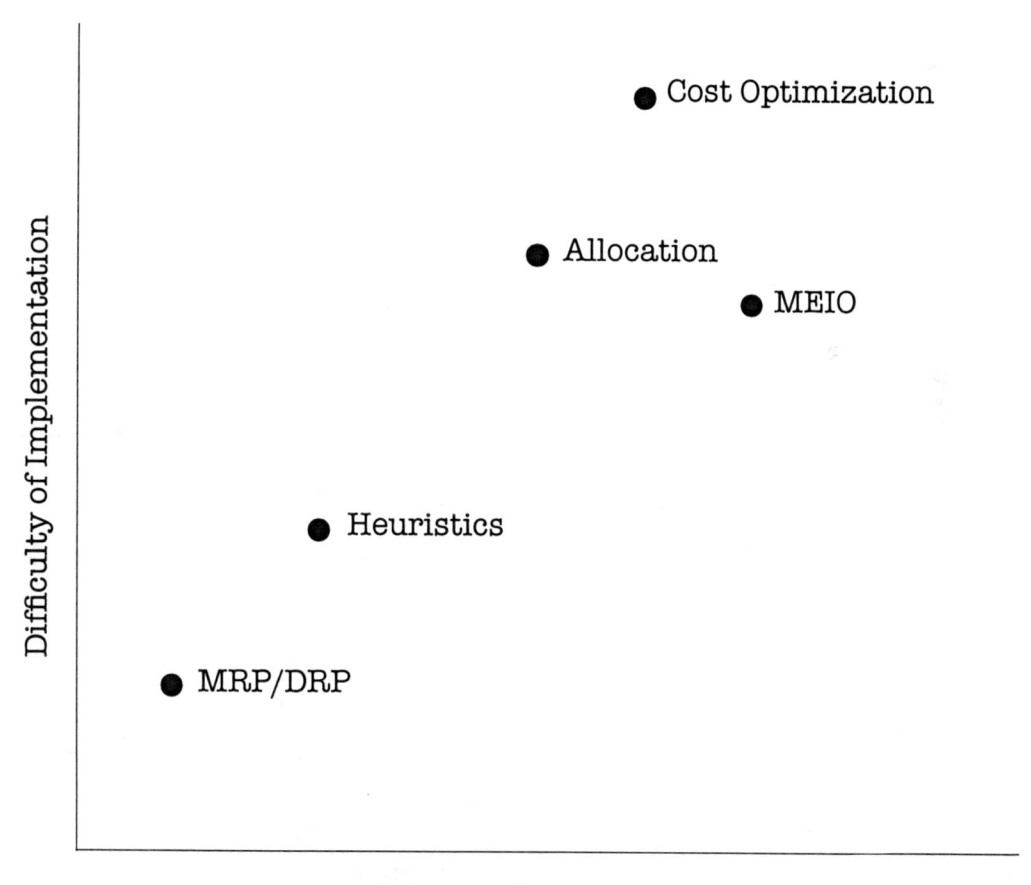

This graphic illustrates the sophistication of the solution versus the difficulty of implementation.

[Chart: Scatter plot with y-axis "Operational Effort to Manage" and x-axis "Configuration / Systems Effort to Manage". Points plotted: MRP/DRP (high y, low x), Heuristics (mid-high y, low-mid x), Cost Optimization (mid y, high x), Allocation (low-mid y, mid-high x), MEIO (low y, mid x).]

This graphic illustrates the operational effort versus configuration and systems effort to manage.

Elaboration on Solution Sophistication Versus Difficulty of Implementation

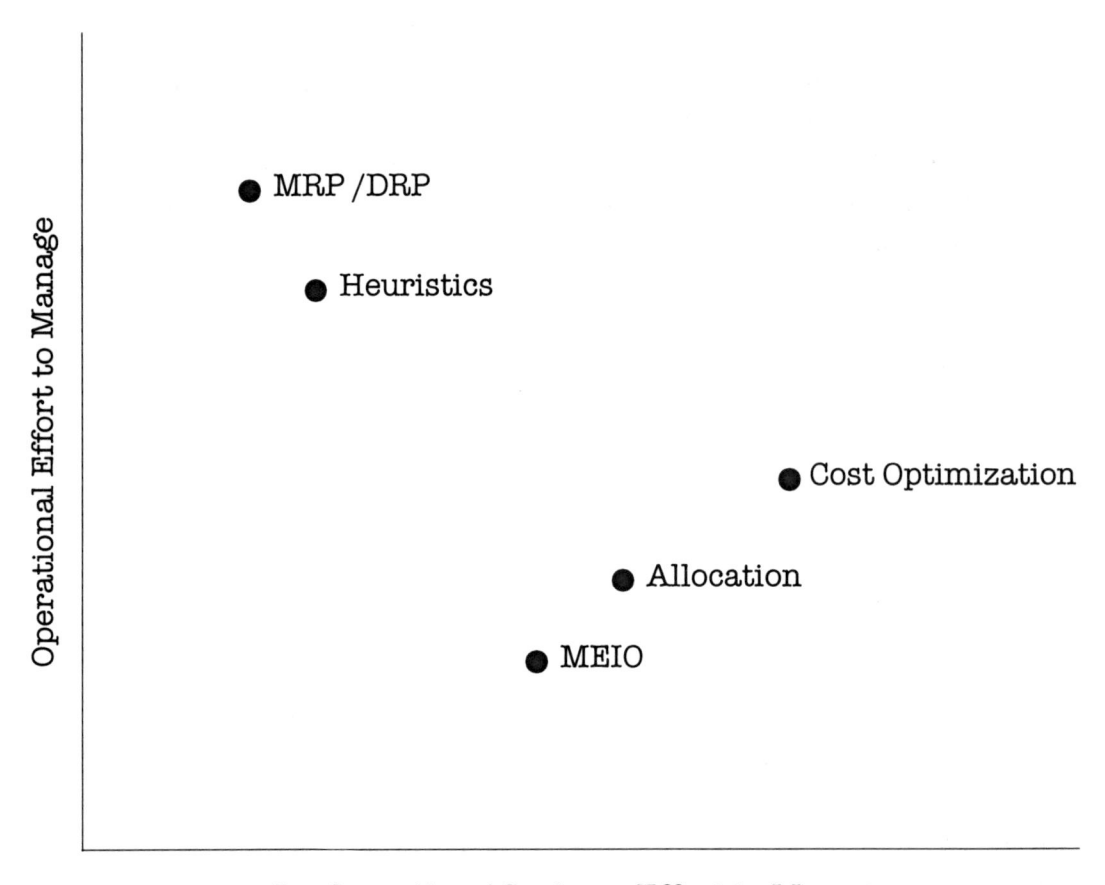

I have rated MEIO as more sophisticated than cost optimization because the mathematics are more sophisticated and more customized for supply planning than cost optimization. This is an important, but mostly overlooked distinction between how various forms of optimization work in practice. For supply planning, transportation planning and even production planning, cost optimization can be considered as the "first generation" attempt to apply optimization to these supply chain domains. There is an implied assumption with any optimization that whatever is used as the objective function is the most important thing to focus on for that particular area. However, in most cases, costs are not the most important thing. Service level tends to be more important for supply planning, and minimizing production durations is normally more important for production planning. Using objective functions, which are customized, per the domain can be understood as the second generation attempts to apply optimization to the supply chain. By customizing optimization in this manner, more thought has been put into each area rather than applying a blanket optimization approach. Interestingly, those companies that have chosen to implement cost optimization often find that cost optimization does not always fit with their objectives. More on this can be found at the link below:

http://www.scmfocus.com/inventoryoptimizationmultiechelon/2011/05/how-costs-are-really-set-in-cost-optimization-implementations/

Furthermore, because cost optimizers are set in a way that prevents the calculation of a global minimum, many of the costs that have been set up in cost optimizers do not actually result in costs being minimized. See the post below for a detailed explanation on this topic.

http://www.scmfocus.com/supplyplanning/2011/07/09/what-is-your-supply-planning-optimizer-optimizing/

How MEIO Compares to the Other Supply Planning Methods With Respect to Long Term Maintenance

As displayed in the graphic on the previous page, there are two dimensions of maintenance in supply planning:

1. System Maintenance

2. Operational Maintenance

System maintenance includes things like changing how the methods run, bringing on new functionality and changing input values. Operational maintenance is the work required by the business to get the system to provide the desired output or to manually override the output.

System Maintenance

MRP and DRP are very basic; in fact, the logic of both is so basic that nothing more than arithmetic is used in either method. (All methods discussed here are considered independently from their planning parameters, as those are universally applied to all the methods.) MRP and DRP have low configuration/system maintenance costs because there is not much to configure or maintain. They are also very easy to troubleshoot, which is an advantage, translating into few controls inherent to the procedure that can be altered (outside of the planning parameters). This can be observed in the settings screenshot below.

Single-Item, Single-Level

Material	SCM Focus Mat	
MRP Area	3800	
Plant	AC00	

MRP control parameters

Processing key	NETCH	Net change for total horizon
Create purchase req.	2	Purchase requisitions in opening period
Delivery schedules	3	Schedule lines
Create MRP list	1	MRP list
Planning mode	1	Adapt planning data (normal mode)
Scheduling	1	Basic dates will be determined for plann
Planning date	27.03.2012	

Process control parameters
☐ Display results before they are saved

This is the MRP screen in SAP ERP, which shows the limited number of options that are available to be set. This compares to the SAP SNP Heuristic, which has a full screen of settings, and to SAP CTM and the SAP SNP Optimizer, both of which have many screens of settings.

Heuristics are not as simple as MRP and DRP, but they tend toward the simpler end of the spectrum both in terms of system and operational maintenance as well as solution sophistication. On the other hand, allocation and cost optimization have historically demonstrated a high enough amount of system maintenance to warrant concern. The amount of system maintenance as well as system analysis effort required to drive to a usable result for allocation and cost optimization has proven simply overwhelming for many companies. I describe this in specific detail in the book *Supply Planning with MRP, DRP and APS Software*.

Operational Maintenance
Operational maintenance—system maintenance that is performed by the business—is the second dimension of maintenance displayed in the above graphic. Due to their lack of sophistication discussed previously, both MRP and DRP provide weak controls over the supply plan and as a result, operational maintenance is high. More manual intervention is required due to the relative imprecision of their service level controls and to their overly simplified location interaction assumptions. The benefits gained from simple procedures in system maintenance are often lost in operational maintenance.

Heuristics, allocation and cost optimization methods are more sophisticated than MRP/DRP, although they maintain the same over-simplified assumption regarding location-to-location interactions (lack of ability to consider inter-related stocking positions) and also have weak service level controls. MEIO offers a very good blend of solution sophistication along with relatively low maintenance for both systems and operations.

Conclusion
The best way to understand the differences between MEIO applications and the other supply planning methods is to understand that their assumptions and mathematical capabilities are inherently different. The differences are quite important, yet generally not well known outside of the MEIO vendors themselves. Two major differences are the location interdependent assumption and the non-sequential processing of the supply network. The differences should be of interest to anyone who concentrates on the technology of supply planning. MEIO applications have

demonstrated, at least through my interaction with them, that a supply planning application can be both sophisticated without imposing excessive burdens in implementation and maintenance efforts and costs. However, I do not want to leave anyone with the impression that MEIO is an easy installation that can be performed without attending to all the details I have laid out thus far. This industry has had far too many promises of easy implementations with enormous upsides that never materialized. Complex applications require technical and managerial intelligence to implement. Even a perfect technology will fail or underperform its potential if implemented incorrectly.

While I would like to say that I have the data on many MEIO accounts to prove that MEIO is in fact lower in maintenance than the other approaches, I unfortunately cannot claim this. I also cannot refer to an organization that maintains this type of research. Generally, while there is always research on new methods that can be applied to supply chain systems, there is little research on what generally makes for successful or unsuccessful implementations. This is demonstrated conclusively from my own research into the history and press coverage of the different supply planning methods. My ratings of MEIO in terms of its long-term maintainability are taken from my observation of the inherent usability, transparency, and simulation capabilities of the MEIO applications with which I have experience.

CHAPTER 10

Conclusion

Objective
I have used this concluding chapter to discuss two topics that I think most people with interests in this area will want to know about after they have completed reading this book:

- The cost/benefit estimation for MEIO.

- The challenges you can expect when attempting to recommend MEIO.

Cost and Benefits Estimation of MEIO
The general costs and benefits of inventory optimization and multi-echelon planning can be used relatively easily to determine if the implementation expense will be worth the predicted cost savings. The costs are of course based on the implementation and maintenance costs that are estimated during the project-planning phase. The cost savings are generally considered to be between ten and twenty percent of inventory. Like any value estimation, this is not a perfect science, as it depends upon a number of assumptions. A few of the assumptions are listed on the following pages.

Assumptions

- The ten to twenty percent figure greatly depends on how well the company is currently managing its inventory and on how well the company will implement and adopt the software into its organization. The reasons why these cost savings are achievable should be evident from understanding how MEIO comes to its planning output differently than other supply planning methods, which is discussed throughout this book.

- The inventory savings are the "hard" savings, but they are not the only savings that can come from MEIO implementations. Instead, the cost savings span improvements such as reduced expedite activities and increased services levels, which tend to lead to greater customer satisfaction and increases in sales volume over the long term. However, these "soft" numbers are more difficult to estimate, so they are not typically included in the analysis.

- The implementation timeline can be as short as six months, but this greatly depends on the client. The implementation timelines of vendors that I work with are not replicated in my personal project experiences. It is easy to stretch out enterprise implementations for a year and a half if requirements are not solid, if data integrity is in question, or if the organization is too overwhelmed by operational concerns to perform a proper implementation. I have seen MEIO implementations that have been live for four years or more and still not delivering much value to the business. This is not because the solution output is incorrect, but because the solution was never explained or socialized properly. Socialization of MEIO concepts and technology is challenging because they are foreign to many supply chain professionals. This has been true of all optimization technologies. (For those who might be interested, I have developed principles for improving the socialization of optimization projects: http://www.scmfocus.com/inventoryoptimization-multiechelon/2011/05/socializing-supply-chain-optimization/.) Additionally, the speed of implementation greatly depends on who is controlling the project. Companies that want a fast MEIO implementation should hand the implementation staffing and management over to the MEIO vendor. I also recommend hiring a non-affiliated independent consultant to provide a third-party perspective. This independent consultant should have a background in MEIO, must be knowledgeable enough to validate or refute statements, explanations and recommendations offered by the vendor and must not be afraid to disagree with the vendor when called for. This independent consultant does not need to be full time. The MEIO vendor consulting resources will be doing most of the configuration of the system, with the role of the independent consultant being quality assurance, solution design (from the broader perspective), application integration and education. The independent consultant's role would obviously vary depending upon his or her skills and the capabilities provided by client resources. This independent consultant should not be subcontracted to the software company or vice versa because of the issue of influence that tends to occur when any one company is the prime contractor. Currently, the skills in inventory optimization and multi-echelon planning are very limited in the major consulting companies as well as the boutique firms. If you choose a large consulting company, you can expect your implementation time and costs to increase substantially. Large consulting companies will expect the vendor consultants to train their consultants, even while both are billing the client for the education of the consulting company resources. Hiring a large consulting company will also mean paying extremely high rates for a partner or director that are not actually doing the work or contributing much to bringing the project live. Furthermore, all of my experience indicates that your likelihood of success will also decrease.

- The selection of the right software is critical to the benefits that can be expected. Not all applications in this space bring the same inventory reduction benefits. I am unaware of any unbiased evidence that one application brings more benefits than another, but the match between the client's needs and the particular vendor selected is a main determining factor of the financial benefits of any MEIO application. Software that may be easier to install can result in lower overall long-term savings. Applications that are more comprehensive can also be implemented with just a portion of their overall functionality. As I have said, there are many differences between MEIO vendors and they will not all implement with the same success in every environment.

The Forces Resisting MEIO

Recommending MEIO is not as easy as one would anticipate given how well it matches with the requirements of many companies. There are many entrenched interests within companies and in consulting firms opposed to MEIO. I have describe this in detail below:

1. Consulting companies that are not familiar with MEIO and are not confident they can control or staff the MEIO projects will tend to minimize the value of MEIO. However, as soon as they can see a revenue stream in MEIO, they will immediately switch to recommending MEIO solutions to their customer base. This will happen as soon as the monopoly enterprise vendors offer MEIO products.

2. Major vendors that do have MEIO applications or pretend to have some MEIO capability significantly lag behind the smaller best-of-breed applications and are, in any case, more experienced and comfortable selling older approaches. The large well-known vendors perceive MEIO as a threat because it is a technology they have nothing to do with. They are doing what they can to co-opt MEIO and convince customers that they were on the leading edge all along. Currently they are attempting to co-opt the smaller vendors with partnerships and promises of more deals, but behind the scenes, they are reverse-engineering their products. As of the publication of this book, none of the major monopoly vendors is within shouting distance of the best-of-breed solutions in MEIO. However, this will not stop the major vendors from claiming their applications are "MEIO-like" or "deal with the multi-echelon problem," or are "similar to MEIO," or that they have a partnership with a MEIO vendor and can sell you accelerators that make the integration a foregone conclusion.

3. MEIO knowledge is not well disseminated within companies or consulting firms, so the benefits of MEIO are generally not well understood. A motivation for this book has been to provide more exposure on MEIO to the general supply chain planning population. My belief is that the more exposure that people have to the many intriguing aspects of MEIO technology, the less resistance to MEIO in the future.

The Opportunity

As I have stated elsewhere, there are a number of high-quality, best-of-breed MEIO solutions to choose from, and supply networks are not nearly as well managed as one would assume from reading supply chain literature. Periodicals tend to promote the concept of continual improvement, but I do not see that in my consulting practice, and there is much more pretend improvement than actual improvement. The discrepancy between the capabilities of supply planning systems and how they are actually used is a yawning chasm. Many advanced supply-planning applications continue to bring major maintenance headaches to companies that have implemented them and force the IT departments to continually fix problems rather than improve and socialize the solution. Supply planning practices in general are far behind the potential that exists, and I have found this to be true at even the largest companies that have very significant resources to apply to systems and process improvements.

Most companies have no precise application for managing their service levels and most do not know that MEIO does exactly this. The opportunities for MEIO are abundant. However, implementation decisions are never simply based on the technological capabilities of a solution. Many other factors are just as important. As a closing note, I am reminded of a conversation I had with a director at one of my clients with whom I had developed a strong relationship. I would repeatedly show her mock-ups of the visibility her department would have if they purchased and implemented the software of a MEIO vendor that I was recommending. In one email, she asked me, "Can I have that?" I responded, "You can if you fight for it."

References

Abell, John B., Louis W. Miller, Curtis E. Neumann, and Judith E. Payne. *DRIVE (Distribution and Repair in Variable Environments)*. RAND Corporation, 1992.

Berners-Lee, Tim. *Weaving the Web: The Original Design and Ultimate Destiny of the World Wide Web*. New York, Harper Paperbacks, 2000.

Cavinato, J.L. and A.J. Stenger. *Adapting MRP to the Outbound Side—Distribution Requirements Planning*. Production and Inventory Management, 1979.

Clark, A.J. *A Dynamic Single-Item, Multi-Echelon Inventory Model*. RAND Corporation, 1958.

Close, A. Frances and Colleen A. Gillen. *Description of the Computer Program for METRIC: A Multi-Echelon Technique for Recoverable Item Control*. RAND Corporation, 1969.

Cohen, M. A., N. Agrawal, and V. Agrawal, "Winning in the Aftermarket." *Harvard Business Review* (May 2006).

Durbin, E. P. and R. D. Wollmer. *Recent Work in Multi-Echelon Inventory Theory*. 1966.

Frontline Solvers, *Optimized Solutions—Distribution Examples,* accessed May 2011, http://www.solver.com/discenter.html

Hillestad, R.J. *Dyna-Metric: Dynamic Multi-Echelon Technique for Recoverable Item Control*. The RAND Corporation, 1982.

Lee, Calvin. *Demand Chain Optimization: Pitfalls and Key Principles.* NONSTOP Solutions, 2002.

Lee, Calvin. "Multi-Echelon Inventory Optimization." *Evant* (2003).

Lei Lei, Shuguang Liu, Andrej Ruszczynski, and Sunju Park. *Integrated Production, Inventory and Distribution Routing Problem.* RUTCOR Research, 2003.

More, Jorge J. and Stephen J. Wright. *Optimization Software Guide.* Society for Industrial and Applied Mathematics, 1993.

Muckstadt, John A. *Analysis and Algorithms for Service Parts Supply Chains.* Springer Press, 2004.

Muckstadt, John A. *Some Approximations in Multi-Item, Multi-Echelon Inventory Systems for Recoverable Items.* RAND Corporation, 1976.

Muckstadt, John A. *The Consolidated Support Model (CSM): A Three Echelon, Multi-Item Model for Recoverable Items.* RAND Corporation, 1976.

Plossl, George. *Production and Inventory Control: Techniques and Principles.* 2nd ed. Prentice Hall, 1985.

Principles of Operations. MCA Solutions.

Project Air Force 1946–1996, RAND Corporation.

Ptak, Carol and Chad Smith. *Orlicky's Material Requirements Planning.* 3rd ed. McGraw Hill Professional, 2011.

Ragsdale, Cliff. *Spreadsheet Modeling & Decision Analysis: A Practical Introduction to Management Science.* 6th ed. South-Western, 2010.

SO99 User Guide. ToolsGroup.

"Service Level Agreement." Wikipedia. Last modified May 2011. http://en.wikipedia.org/wiki/Service_level_agreement

Sherbrooke, Craig C. "METRIC: A Multi-Echelon Technique for Recoverable Item Control." *Operations Research* 16 (1968).

Sherbrooke, C.C. *Multi-Echelon, Multi-Item Inventory Model for Recoverable Items.* RAND Corporation, 1966.

Sherbrooke, C.C. *METRIC: A Multi-Echelon Technique for Recoverable Item Control.* RAND Corporation, 1966.

Snapp, Shaun. *Supply Planning with MRP, DRP and APS Software.* SCM Focus Press, 2012.

"Non Linear Programming." Wikipedia. Last modified December 2011
http://en.wikipedia.org/wiki/Nonlinear_programming

"Simplex Algorithm." Wikipedia. Last Modified January 2012.
http://en.wikipedia.org/wiki/Simplex_algorithm

"Linear Programming." Wikipedia. Last Modified January 2012.
http://en.wikipedia.org/wiki/Linear_programming

"Simulation Software." Wikipedia. Last Modified January 2012.
http://en.wikipedia.org/wiki/Simulation_software

"Simulated Annealing." Wikipedia. Last Modified January 2012.
http://en.wikipedia.org/wiki/Simulated_annealing

"Supply Chain Optimization." Wikipedia. Last Modified November 2011.
http://en.wikipedia.org/wiki/Supply_chain_optimization

"Tim Berners-Lee." Wikipedia. Last Modified January 2012.
http://en.wikipedia.org/wiki/Tim_Berners-Lee

Most Expensive Cars to Repair. Jacqueline Mitchell.
http://www.forbes.com/2008/05/05/cars-expensive-repairs-forbeslife-cx_jm_0505cars.html

The following links are to manuals for the IBM 704. The machine was interesting in that both FORTRAN and LISP languages were first developed for the 704. It was also the first computer to synthesize speech. The 704 manual declares "production scheduling and control, econometrics, logistics, procurement and supply" and problems which could be solved with it.

http://www.cs.virginia.edu/brochure/images/manuals/IBM_704/IBM_704.html

Fortran Reference Manual. 1956.
http://www.fortran.com/FortranForTheIBM704.pdf

Cullinan, Charles, Steve G. Sutton and Vicky Arnold. *Technology Monoculture: ERP Systems.* Bingley, UK. Emerald Publishing Group Limited, 2010

Cohen, Morris, Pasumarti V. Kamesam, Paul Kleindorfer, Hau Lee, and Armen Tekerian. *Optimizer: IBM's Multi-Echelon Inventory System for Managing Service Logistics.* Institute of Management Sciences, 1990.

"Lean Construction." Wikipedia. Last Modified January 2012.
http://en.wikipedia.org/wiki/Lean_construction

Vendor Acknowledgements and Profiles

I have listed brief profiles of each vendor with screen shots included in this book below.

ToolsGroup

ToolsGroup offers unique probability-based supply chain planning (SCP) and inventory optimization solutions that allow companies to master even large, heterogeneous, or demanding supply chains. On the demand side, they incorporate best-of-breed demand modeling, order frequency forecasting, and demand-sensing technology. On the supply side, they offer multi-echelon inventory optimization and replenishment planning.

   http://www.toolsgroup.com

Logility

Logility is a leading provider of collaborative, best-of-breed supply chain solutions that helps small, medium, large, and Fortune 1000 companies realize substantial bottom-line results in record time. Logility Voyager Solutions is a complete supply chain management solution that features performance-monitoring capabilities in a single

Internet-based framework and provides supply chain visibility, demand, inventory, and replenishment planning.

http://www.logility.com

Servigistics

Servigistics is the world's leading enterprise software solution provider for Service Lifecycle Management (SLM). The company's award-winning SLM solutions suite enables market-leading companies across diverse industries to successfully execute a service-led growth strategy that delivers value across the entire global service supply chain. Servigistics' solutions address all the key post-sales service areas including service parts planning and pricing, field service management, service logistics, warranty management, service knowledge, remote service and content management.

http://www.servigistics[3]

SmartOps

SmartOps, the market leader in enterprise-class supply chain optimization solutions, enables companies to manage the uncertainty of complex, multistage supply chains to achieve a rapid return on investment and long-term, sustainable value.

http://www.smartops.com

*The SAP screenshots in the book are not MEIO screenshots as they are not a MEIO vendor. The screen shots I have used from SAP are used to describe heuristics, MRP that are compared to MEIO, but are unrelated to MEIO. I have not included SAP's profile because I do not want readers who casually glance at this page to think that SAP offers a MEIO application. All screen shots are covered under US fair use law.

---

[3] While this book was being written, Servigistics acquired MCA Solutions. According to Mark Vigoroso, the SVP of Global Marketing and Alliances at Servigistics, "We will be doing one more version upgrade for MCA clients (to version 8). But the strategy will be to consolidate the best of Servigistics and MCA into a single platform going forward. We will not have separate SPM applications (e.g. the MCA solution, the Servigistics solution)."

On some most occasions I refer to the MCA Solutions product acquired as the Servigistics product. However, in other cases, such as when I refer to something that occurred in the past, I refer to MCA Solutions.

Author Profile

Shaun Snapp is the managing editor of SCM Focus. SCM Focus is one of the largest independent supply chain software analysis and educational sites on the Internet.

After working at several of the largest consulting companies and at i2 Technologies, he became an independent consultant and later started SCM Focus. He maintains a strong interest in comparative software design, and works both in SAP APO, as well as with a variety of best-of-breed supply chain planning vendors. His ongoing relationships with these vendors keep him on the cutting edge of emerging technology.

Primary Sources of Information and Writing Topics

Shaun writes about topics with which he has first-hand experience. These topics range from recovering problematic implementations, to system configuration, to socializing complex software and supply chain concepts in the areas of demand planning, supply planning and production planning.

More broadly, he writes on topics supportive of these applications, which include master data parameter management, integration, analytics, simulation and bill of material management systems. He covers management aspects of enterprise software ranging from software policy to handling consulting partners on SAP projects.

Shaun writes from an implementer's perspective and as a result he focuses on how software is actually used in practice rather than its hypothetical or "pure release note capabilities." Unlike many authors in enterprise software who keep their distance from discussing the realities of software implementation, he writes both on the problems as well as the successes of his software use. This gives him a distinctive voice in the field.

Secondary Sources of Information

In addition to project experience, Shaun's interest in academic literature is a secondary source of information for his books and articles. Intrigued with the historical perspective of supply chain software, much of his writing is influenced by his readings and research into how different categories of supply chain software developed, evolved and finally became broadly used over time.

Covering the Latest Software Developments

Shaun is focused on supply chain software selections and implementation improvement through writing and consulting, bringing companies some of the newest technologies and methods. Some of the software developments that Shaun showcases at SCM Focus and in books at SCM Focus Press have yet to reach widespread adoption.

Education

Shaun has an undergraduate degree in business from the University of Hawaii, a Masters of Science in Maritime Management from the Maine Maritime Academy and a Masters of Science in Business Logistics from Penn State University. He has taught both logistics and SAP software.

Software Certifications
Shaun has been trained and/or certified in products from i2 Technologies, Servigistics, ToolsGroup and SAP (SD, DP, SNP, SPP, EWM).

Contact
Shaun can be contacted at:
shaunsnapp@scmfocus.com

Abbreviations

APS – Advanced Planning and Scheduling

CTM – Capable to Match

DBA – Database Administrator

DC – Distribution Center

DRP – Distribution Requirements Planning

ERP – Enterprise Resource Planning

ISL – Initial Stocking Level

MEIO – Inventory Optimization and Multi-Echelon Planning

MRP – Materials Requirements Planning

RDC – Regional Distribution Center

SLA – Service Level Agreement

SNP – Supply Network Planning (a product made by SAP which is part of the SCM/APO suite)

S&OP – Sales and Operations Planning

SQL – Structure Query Language

TSL – Target Stocking Level

Links in the Book

Chapter 1

http://www.scmfocus.com/inventoryoptimizationmultiechelon/2010/10/booz-allen-hamilton-misrepresents-inventory-optimization-in-white-papers/

Chapter 2

http://www.scmfocus.com/supplyplanning/2011/07/10/customizing-the-optimization-per-supply-chain-domain/

Chapter 3

http://www.scmfocus.com/inventoryoptimizationmultiechelon/2010/04/inventory-optimization-definition/

http://www.scmfocus.com/inventoryoptimizationmultiechelon/2010/01/inventory-optimization-flexibility-and-the-service-level-hierarchy/

http://www.scmfocus.com/supplychainsimulation/2011/10/12/understanding-the-difference-between-enterprise-optimizers-and-modeling-languages/

http://www.scmfocus.com/meiobook/files/2010/10/TSL_or_SS.jpg.

http://www.scmfocus.com/inventoryoptimizationmultiechelon/2011/03/why-safety-stock-is-not-the-focus-of-inventory-optimization/

http://www.scmfocus.com/meiobook/files/2010/10/TSL_or_SS.jpg.

http://www.scmfocus.com/supplyplanning/2011/07/24/why-the-cost-of-missed-demand-must-alway-be-set-so-much-higher-than-the-profit-margin/

http://www.scmfocus.com/inventoryoptimizationmultiechelon/2010/01/inventory-optimization-flexibility-and-the-service-level-hierarchy/

http://www.scmfocus.com/inventoryoptimizationmultiechelon/2010/01/inventory-optimization-flexibility-and-the-service-level-hierarchy/

http://www.scmfocus.com/enterprisesoftwarepolicy/2012/01/27/how-common-is-it-for-sap-to-take-intellectual-property-from-partners/

http://www.scmfocus.com/inventoryoptimizationmultiechelon/2010/11/segmentation-vs-inventory-optimization/

Chapter 4

http://www.scmfocus.com/inventoryoptimizationmultiechelon/2010/01/effective-lead-time-and-multi-echelon/

http://www.scmfocus.com/supplyplanning/2011/07/17/considering-the-probability-of-success-of-different-aps-methods-for-supply-planning/

http://www.scmfocus.com/sapplanning/2011/11/05/how-soft-constraints-work-with-soft-constraints-days-supply-and-safety-stock-penalty-costs/

Chapter 5

http://www.scmfocus.com/inventoryoptimizationmultiechelon/2011/10/redeployment/

http://www.scmfocus.com/sapplanning/2011/10/12/snp-optimizer-sub-problem-division-and-decomposition/

Chapter 6

http://www.scmfocus.com/supplyplanning/2011/07/17/considering-the-probability-of-success-of-different-aps-methods-for-supply-planning/

http://www.scmfocus.com/supplyplanning/2011/07/24/why-the-cost-of-missed-demand-must-alway-be-set-so-much-higher-than-the-profit-margin/

http://www.scmfocus.com/supplyplanning/2011/10/02/commonly-used-and-unused-constraints-for-supply-planning/

http://www.scmfocus.com/sapplanning/2009/07/01/bottleneck-resources/

http://www.scmfocus.com/productionplanningandscheduling/2011/03/29/why-mixing-operations-can-be-appropriate-for-weak-production-scheduling-applications/

http://www.scmfocus.com/inventoryoptimizationmultiechelon/2010/01/inventory-optimization-flexibility-and-the-service-level-hierarchy/

Chapter 7

http://www.scmfocus.com/inventoryoptimizationmultiechelon/2011/10/using-meio-to-connect-sales-and-supply-chain-planning/

http://www.vimeo.com/15060562

http://www.scmfocus.com/supplychainsimulation/

Chapter 8

http://www.scmfocus.com/sapplanning/2009/12/08/customer-prioritization-and-ctm/

http://www.vimeo.com/15101084

http://www.scmfocus.com/supplychaininnovation/2010/10/eric-larkin-and-nathan-martin-from-arena-solutions-on-the-benefits-of-saas/

http://www.cisco.com/en/US/products/ps6602/products_ios_protocol_group_home.html

http://www.google.com/apps/intl/en/terms/sla.html

http://www.sun.com/blueprints/0402/sla.pdf

Chapter 9

http://www.vimeo.com/15101084

http://www.scmfocus.com/sapplanning/2011/10/12/snp-optimizer-sub-problem-division-and-decomposition/

http://www.scmfocus.com/supplyplanning/2011/07/09/what-is-your-supply-planning-optimizer-optimizing/

http://www.scmfocus.com/supplyplanning/2011/07/09/what-is-your-supply-planning-optimizer-optimizing/

Chapter 10

http://www.scmfocus.com/inventoryoptimizationmultiechelon/2011/05/socializing-supply-chain-optimization/

Appendix A: MEIO Visibility and Analytics

As was described in Chapter 7: "MEIO and Simulation," visibility supports a strong simulation capability and is a major component of many MEIO applications. Analytics are essentially an aggregated view of the application and is designed for executives, whereas most MEIO user interfaces are designed for planners.

Different Approaches to Visibility

One of the most interesting aspects of evaluating software from different MEIO vendors is seeing how they address the issue of providing visibility to the user. While the underlying technology among vendors can be unique or can overlap, interface design concepts and how data is displayed are consistently different between the various vendors. Because of these differences, I have gradually come to the viewpoint that companies must intimately work with and understand the applications in order to pick the solution that best fits their needs. Understanding the underlying technical differences between vendors is critical to decision-making, but matching the interface design to the preferences and aptitudes of the user community is also important and, certainly underemphasized. Showing each application to all potential users is a quick and effective way to get feedback on which application would have the highest potential for adoption. The eventual users should have the opportunity to interact with the provider of the demo from the vendor and, even, to get hands-on experience with the application. If this extends the demo to several hours, that should not be a concern. The application that the company chooses should really have the users saying they "have to have it." When users make those types of statements, the system is already on a better path for a successful implementation.

MEIO and Analytics

MEIO software, up until recently, was almost exclusively used and reviewed by planners. MEIO applications primarily interacted with executive decision makers only through reports. That is no longer the case. A number of MEIO vendors have added analytics products or dashboards to their main MEIO planning engine, something I consider a natural extension of MEIO applications. It is too early to know how successful these analytics front ends will be, but several that I have seen look promising. Below is a screenshot from the analytics front end for SmartOps.

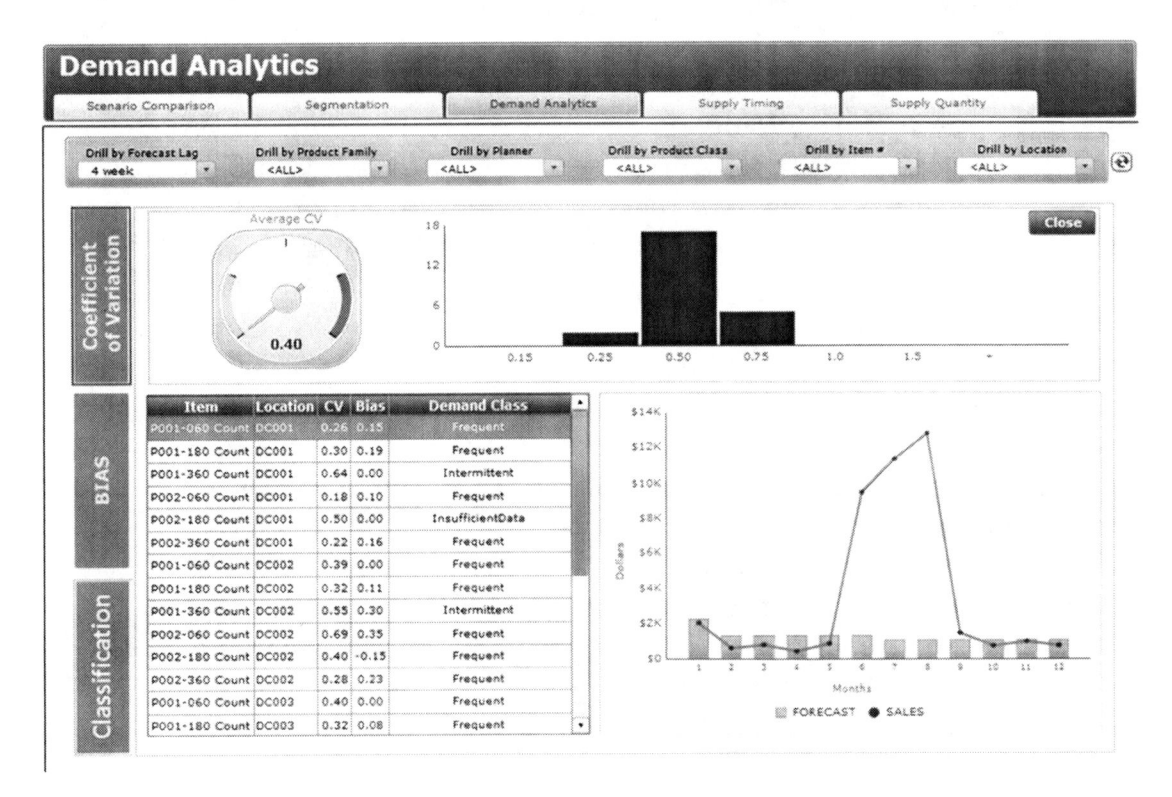

There are several tabs in this interface; on the previous page is the Demand Analytics tab, which interprets demand history versus the forecast to support better forecasting prior to using the forecast in the supply planning MEIO application. These types of front ends not only improve the understanding of the application, but also expand the user base to include management and executive ranks, as well as planners. It allows the MEIO vendor to package similar reporting requirements across different clients and to offer frequently requested views.

Appendix B: The History of Development of MEIO Versus MRP/DRP

One of the most interesting stories regarding multi-echelon planning and inventory optimization is when these methods were developed, when they were published and when they were placed into enterprise software and became broadly, commercially used. The timeline below was developed by comparing when the first research papers were created in the various supply planning topic versus when the methods began to find broad application.

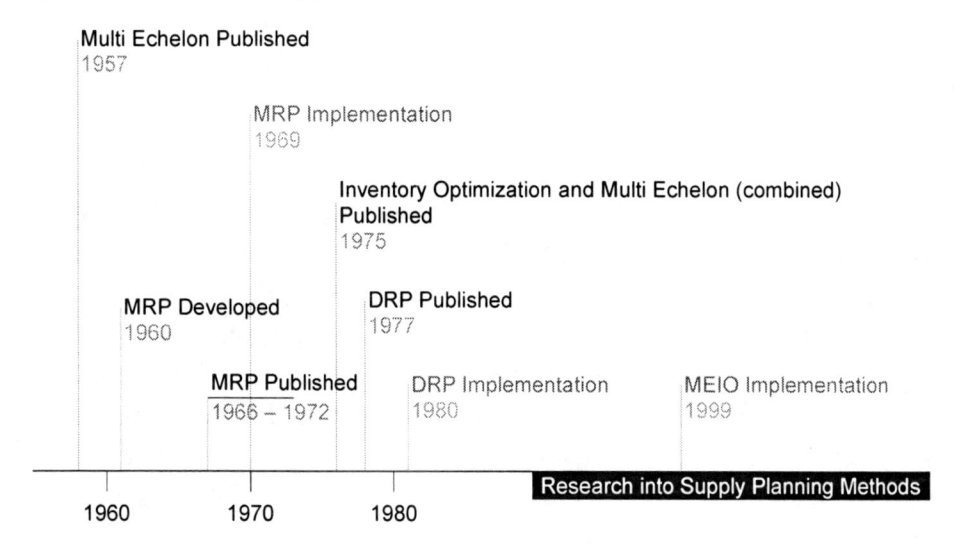

Multi Echelon Published
1957

MRP Implementation
1969

Inventory Optimization and Multi Echelon (combined) Published
1975

MRP Developed
1960

DRP Published
1977

MRP Published
1966 – 1972

DRP Implementation
1980

MEIO Implementation
1999

Research into Supply Planning Methods

1960   1970   1980

165

The Lag Between Initial Development, Publication and Commercialization

Something, which is made very apparent from this timeline is that the simpler methods, such as MRP and DRP had a much smaller lag between their development and their commercialization and general implementation. Research into advanced methods such as multi-echelon planning actually preceded MRP by several years, but while MRP was broadly implemented within ten years of its initial development, multi-echelon would take another forty years after its initial development until it would be broadly used in commercial applications. This brings up interesting questions as to why the lag was so large for MEIO. The answer is clearly that simpler methods, while leaving out important functionality, are easier to write software for, and easier to implement. A second reason is that MEIO method development predated their ability to be used in computers. The early tests, such as A.J. Clark's multi-echelon model were far head of the computational capabilities at the time. Therefore, they could only be modeled in a very oversimplified way. A.J. Clark's early paper tested his mathematics with only a single material in order to cut down on computation time. However, as a chart further on in this appendix will show, the computing capability eventually did become available to use the more advanced methods, but they still weren't used until sometime after this. If MEIO is such a good thing, the natural question is why not? Why did MEIO have to wait until roughly 2000 until it was commercialized?

The paper "George B. Dantzig and Systems Optimization" may provide part of the answer.

> Unfortunately for the nascent Stanford SOL (Systems Optimization Laboratory), in those days United States government agencies were reluctant to fund software development, which was not considered to be fundamental research. GBD nonetheless continued in his low-key but persistent way to seek and obtain funding to establish an SOL. The authors of this paper believe that it is now safe to reveal that he managed to do so by bootstrapping grants in optimization that emphasized mathematical theory without mentioning any of the software-related activities that he planned to include.

Therefore, while the US government was willing to fund research into the development of mathematical methods for supply chain planning (among many other endeavors), they were unwilling to fund software development that could have made these innovative methods usable. The researchers themselves knew that they needed to prototype their mathematics with software, so they went forward with building software models of MEIO. If the US Government had understood the need to fund software development as well as mathematical theory, it is likely that more advanced supply planning methods would have come to play in supply planning much earlier than they did. However, when we cover why the initial research into MEIO was performed, it becomes confusing as to why the government did not support software development.

Do Academics Primarily Follow the Lead of Practitioners?

Methods tend not to be "created" by just one person. With MRP, the individuals who are most commonly credited with the development of MRP are Joe Orlicky, George Plossl and Ollie Wight, with Joe Orlicky being seen as the primary developer. MRP was first introduced in industry before it was a published topic. In fact, MRP does not begin showing up in articles until the early 1970s. Orlicky himself wrote one of the major articles in 1973 and George Plossl wrote a book, with Orlicky's input, describing "Orlicky's MRP" which was published in 1975. DRP followed a similar path of being commercialized first, and then published second. I am not the first to observe that MRP developed not by academics but by practitioners. This quote is from Orlicky and is from the 1975 book, *Orlicky's Material Requirements Planning*.

> The techniques of modern material requirements planning has been developed not by theoreticians and researchers but by practitioners. Generally, academia continues to research and write about what is already written rather than developing new insights and thought leadership. The practitioners who use technology and techniques remain in the best position to properly and practically define the tool and techniques that actually produce sustainable positive results.

While it is clear that practitioners developed MRP and DRP (which is essentially a modification of MRP), Orlicky's is not correct that this example generalizes to other supply planning innovations. Quite the opposite of Orlicky's quotation, academics tend to be very much forward looking. In fact, most academic research is so forward looking that in order to get articles published academic researchers are generally promoted by department heads to produce new concepts, and not review how old concepts fared in practice. I consider this unfortunate as reviewing past implementation of a concept is also quite important. However, the fact is that most of the publications that I review in this area discuss new things, and rarely are reviews of older methods. Researchers I have spoken to in a variety of fields declare this consistent orientation. This unfortunately means that methods are proposed, but little research funding is available to evaluate how those methods performed. Reviewing the performance of older techniques is not how researchers make a name for themselves. It is considered to be "not original" research.

In a rare research paper in this area that did take a historical view, "George B. Dantzig and Systems Optimization," was not original research, but still extremely valuable and an important contribution to my understanding of the progression of optimization. George B. Dantzig, due to his prominence at the time, had the luxury of getting this type of paper published, which may have not been published if submitted by a less prominent academic. In fact, many of the papers I reviewed that were written in the 1950s and 1970s described methods for which the computational power did not exist to implement at the time. That is how forward looking or "theoretical" is much of academic research. Therefore, MRP and DRP should be seen as exceptions to the rule that academics in production and inventory management tend to lead rather than follow.

Was the Information on MRP Kept Secret for Commercial Reasons?

Joe Orlicky has the following to say on this topic:

> Thus the knowledge remained for a long time, the property of scattered MRP system users who normally have little time or inclination to write for the public.

Orlickey is correct in this assertion. The fact that MRP and DRP were first implemented and then later published in order to maintain commercial advantage meant that the methods could not be improved upon by larger groups of specialists in this area before they became solidified in method and within software applications. However, this was an unfortunate rather than positive aspect of the development of MRP and DRP. In other areas of innovation, when the originators of an important development keeps the basic formula to themselves they tend to become wealthy, but the overall concept does not advance as it could have and the collective good is reduced. Sharing research information is the heart of the academic publication concept. When the originator shares the information and pushes for standards, as did Tim Berners-Lee when he developed HTML and hyper linking, much more overall utility is created, although the originator does not become as wealthy.

Computational Limitations and MEIO

It should be noted that in the early 1960s, computers were just powerful enough to process MRP logic for entire product databases, and were not nearly powerful enough to process inventory optimization logic for entire product databases. In the 1958 testing that was performed at the RAND Corporation, use of a *single product*, rather than multiple products or an entire product database were tested with the software, and this was done, as stated explicitly in the research paper, to reduce computational time. This provides insight into the hardware limitations at the time. Several methods were developed prior to and after MRP's development that held more accurate assumptions than MRP. However, higher accuracy also meant more complexity and required more computation. Therefore, they would always be more complex to both compute, more difficult to place into enterprise software as well as more complex to implement. Contrary to what is commonly believed, the fact that most of the major supply planning methods are over-simplified models of the supply chain network and how products and location interact with one another has been known by specialists for as long as these methods have been used. This was well understood by researchers in this area as of course far more sophisticated research papers pre-date the development of less sophisticated methods like MRP and DRP. A.J. Clark makes this clear back in 1958 when he writes:

> Recent work has incorporated demand uncertainty expressed in probability distributions, with parameters as functions of time to allow for a changing future. Models of this kind may be called ***dynamic, single-item, single-echelon inventory models.*** Real world systems

are often more complex, of course, since many contain several echelons and regenerate failed parts through repair."

MEIO Development and RAND

Universities did not initially develop MEIO, although they extended MEIO with later research. Instead a single government-sponsored research institute initially developed MEIO. A great deal of credit should go to the US Air Force for both asking difficult questions and funding long-range research into advanced methods like cost optimization, multi-echelon planning and inventory optimization. The Air Force was an important funding source for other areas of innovation in operations research. For instance, the US Air Force was instrumental in funding other research areas such as the development of the simplex method for solving linear programs.

The US Air Force provided the funding and the problem statement, but the work was performed and published through the RAND Corporation in Santa Monica, California.[4,5] Furthermore, several of the main researchers such as John A. Muckstadt were also consultants for the Air Force, and the Office of Naval Research and used Air Force supply chain information for the modeling. Major funding for the early papers by A.J. Clark, Craig C. Sherbrooke and John A. Muckstadt were all funded by this same combination of the Air Force through the RAND Corporation. Furthermore, this funding continued from late 1950s to the late 1970s. Quite interestingly, most of focus of inventory optimization and multi-echelon research was directed toward service parts planning, not toward finished goods planning. This is because the Air Force was attempting to solve its own service parts planning issues. The service parts planning problem is the most difficult to solve from both the demand planning and supply planning perspectives.

According to their fifty year retrospective of "Project Air Force," (of which MEIO research was one component) RAND had up to sixty analysts working on logistics research over a fifty year period. Their initiative was large enough that they created the Logistics System Laboratory. This research was predominantly in two areas:

---

[4] "RAND" is simply a concatenation of Research And Development
[5] RAND is not a university, but publishes research and offers graduate degrees in policy studies, and in many ways functions as a university, except it does not provide undergraduate education.

- Spare parts policies: including studies of aircraft maintenance management at base, depot, inventory theory, spares and repair management and reliability of aircraft avionics systems.
- Increasing the flexibility and responsiveness in the entire logistics system to help mitigate the impossibility of forecasting resource demands with any precision.

This research is considered quite successful in retrospect. According to RAND's own public documentation, they consider the related research of Sherbrook's (and others) METRIC to be one of the top achievements of the Logistics System Laboratory, and Dyna-Metric to be another. CLOUT (Coupling Logistics to Operations to meet Uncertainties and the Threat) was another high profile research initiative that promoted the following:

1. (It) urged the Air Force to rely less on large warehouses of assets based on poor forecasts and to rely more on rapid resupply from depot repair and on lateral repair and supply.
2. The study focused on wartime induced uncertainties and demonstrated both the necessity and the cost effectiveness of investing in a small fleet of aircraft dedicated to moving spare parts quickly among the bases of the European theater. These findings led to the establishment of the European Distribution System.

A.J. Clark and the Processing Power Required for MEIO

A.J. Clark's work, "A Dynamic, Single-Item, Multi-Echelon Inventory Model" is the first paper that I can find on multi-echelon inventory optimization. His paper is primarily focused on service parts and is an amazing work that was at least a decade ahead of its time. A.J. Clark directly discussed the computational problems with respect to the mathematics that he had developed.

> The multi-echelon problem is conceptually a multi-dimensional dynamic programming problem. Such problems, however, are computationally unfeasible for more than two or three dimensions even with electronic computers. To avoid this difficulty, the problem was converted to a set

of interconnected one-dimensional problems by using artifices and imposing certain restrictive assumptions.

That means A.J. Clark and others that worked with him were modeling five echelon supply networks with the following characteristics:

1. Thirty bases (locations)
2. The model processed only a single item
3. Eighteen periods in the production lead-time
4. Six periods in the repair cycle
5. All probability distributions were internally computed with a choice of Poisson, Negative Binomial, or Normal designated by inputs.
6. Twenty-three interconnected one-dimensional dynamic programming problems
7. Included production setup costs

The Processing Power that Was Used
We are lucky enough to have A.J. Clark describe not only the modeled problem, but also the computer that was used to perform the computation. This is a detail that usually seems insignificant at the time of the paper's publication, but which becomes increasingly of interest as time passes. He describes the computer that was used in the quotation below:

> A version of this model has been programmed for the IBM 704 at the RAND Corporation.

The IBM 704 was the first mass produced computer with floating point arithmetic hardware and was first introduced in 1954. It was capable of executing 40,000 instructions per second. RAND had one of the 123 704 systems that were sold from 1955 to 1960. As a point of comparison, by 1974 an Intel 8080 was capable of 500 thousand instructions per second. In 1982, an Intel 286 processor was capable of 2.66 million instructions per second. In 2011, an Intel Core i7 990x was capable of 159,000 million instructions per second. The improvement in computational power is displayed in the following graphic:

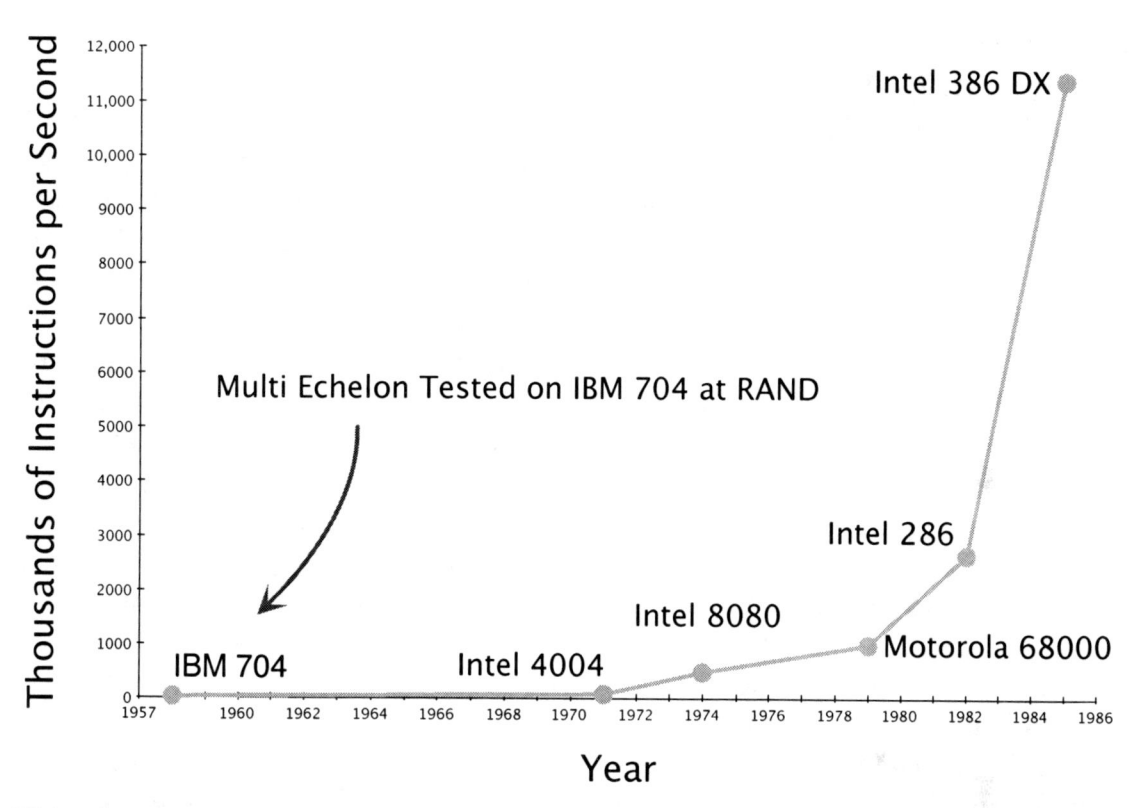

Appendix B: The History of Development of MEIO Versus MRP/DRP

[Chart: Thousands of Instructions per Second vs Year (1957–1986)
- IBM 704 (1957) — Multi Echelon Tested on IBM 704 at RAND
- Intel 4004 (1971)
- Intel 8080 (1974)
- Motorola 68000 (1979)
- Intel 286 (1982)
- Intel 386 DX (1985)]

This chart stops at 1986, because to add more data points after that period would make the magnitude of the earlier data points imperceptible. However, there is another relationship which is not shown in this graphic, but which should be recognized. This is the price of the different hardware that is used as data points. The first data point is the IBM 704. This was a specialized computer designed for engineering and scientific calculation. The computer filled a large room and was connected to multiple printers, at least four tape drives (and up to ten), a magnetic drum all as big as refrigerators, and a dot matrix printer, card punch and (punched) card reader all around the size of present-day washing machines. Only 123 IBM 704s were ever purchased over a six-year period, and only universities and government supported research institutions tended to buy them. Meanwhile, the later data points are processors that were sold as part of personal computers. Therefore, the cost-to-performance chart would be even more impressive than this graphic.

Chart developed with data from Wikipedia: http://en.wikipedia.org/wiki/Instructions_per_second

Conclusion

Research into the publication of new supply planning methods versus when the methods were broadly commercialized in software shows that MRP and DRP were developed first, and published second. MRP, particularly, was not published by those that could have at the time because the wanted to keep the information to themselves as they were engaged in consulting or with software development and wanted to better compete in the marketplace. Simpler supply planning techniques were commercialized much more quickly than the more complex techniques. Several reasons combined to limit the use of MEIO in supply planning until roughly four decades after the earliest papers on the topic began to appear. There are, in fact, several reasons for such a large lag between MEIO's initial development and its incorporation into commercial software packages. For some time, the computational abilities available with hardware were simply not ready for the MEIO for production volumes. Secondly, there is a limited ability within companies to absorb various methods and this is true across all the supply chain planning domains. Investing in one method necessarily reduces the appetite for implementing other methods. Simply implementing MRP and DRP consumed the implementation "bandwidth" for supply planning systems improvement at companies for some time. Companies did not begin incorporating advanced planning for supply planning until the 1990s. Therefore, MRP became entrenched prior to MEIO being placed into commercially available applications. The most controllable factor was the orientation of the US Government to not fund software development. This is a little known factor that played a decisive role in the course that MEIO took. If the US Government had followed an alternate policy, there is a strong likelihood that MEIO could have been implemented in software much sooner and industry may not have standardized so completely around MRP and DRP. The study of the development of these methods is a very interesting topic that holds important lessons for software development, innovation, government versus private research and how new approaches transition from research environments to practical implementation.

Index

Advanced Planning and Strategy (APS), 31–2, 63, 80, 127–8, 129
Air Force, U.S., 170
alerts, interface design and, 75–6
allocation method, 47, 133–4, 137
analytics, 162–3
automotive service supply chains, example of, 50–2

Berners-Lee, Tim, 169
Bullwhip Effect, 45

change management, 62
Cisco, 117
Clark, A.J., 38, 166, 169–72
CLOUT, 171
computational limitations, 169–72
constraint-based planning, 88–91, 97
consulting companies, 2, 4, 33–4, 50, 92, 140–2
Consumer Reports, 52
contract, service level set at, 46, 57

cost optimization
    appropriateness of, 10–11
    basic function of, 82–3
    common problems with, 86–9, 92, 97–8
    constraint-based planning and, 88–91, 97
    decomposition in, 130–2
    defined in terms of goal, 82
    failure to understand, 84–6
    MEIO vs., 77–98
    multi-sourcing and, 90–2
    operational vs. configuration/ systems effort to manage and, 134–7
    ranking recommendations and, 73
    service level and, 93–4
    solution sophistication vs. implementation difficulty and, 133–5
cost optimizers, 62, 101–2
CPLEX, 20

customer, service level set at, 56, 58–9
customer service. See service level.
customization of optimization, 10–11
cycle stock, 32

Dantzig, George B., 168
Data Base Administrators (DBAs), 103–4
data flow, MEIO and, 12–13
Daugherty, Rod, 70
days' supply, 60–2, 64, 118
decomposition, 73, 130–2
demand planning, MEIO applications and, 8–9
deployment, 37
distribution centers, multi-echelon networks and, 41–3, 45–8
Distribution Requirements Planning (DRP), 31, 40, 47, 63, 89, 127–8, 129–30, 133–4, 136–7, 165–70, 174
durations, optimization and, 10, 78, 82, 84–5, 132
Dyna-Metric, 171
dynamic safety stock, 21–3, 31–2, 118

"echelon," meaning of, 378
enterprise optimization solutions, general optimizers solvers vs., 17–21
Enterprise Resource Planning (ERP) system, 13, 21, 32, 72, 100
European Distribution System, 171
exception-based management planning, 75–6
explicit costs, 83–4, 87

facility capacity, safety stock and, 24
fair share distribution, 130
finite planning. See constraint based planning.

general optimizers solvers, enterprise optimization solutions vs., 17–21
Google Apps, 117
group location, service levels set at, 54–5

heuristics, 47, 89, 129–30, 133–4, 137

IBM 704, 172–3
implementation of MEIO, 97–8, 138, 140–1
implicit costs, 83–4, 87, 93–4, 98
incremental pricing, 120–1
independent consultants, 140–1
independent planning, 44
initial stocking level, 21–3
integration of systems, 12
inventory balancing. See redeployment.
inventory optimization
    sub-branch of mathematical optimization, 15–16, 34
    first combined with multi-echelon, 37
    mathematics of, 15–16, 71
    relation to multi-echelon, 39, 65–76
    segmentation and, 32–3
    target stocking level and, 21–2, 34
    cost optimization vs., 77–8, 97
    defined, 16, 34
    basics of, 7, 16, 34, 39, 66, 76
inventory service level specificity, 16
IT departments, 85, 88, 143

Larkin, Erik, 116
lead times
    effective, 45, 47–50, 58, 67–9
    static, 48
Lee, Calvin, 30, 43–5, 58
location independence, 128–9

location interdependence, 39–40, 128–9, 137
location, service level set at, 54–5
Logility, 27, 95, 107–8, 149–50
Logistics System Laboratory, 170–1
long-term maintenance, 134–7

Manhattan Associates, 70
Martin, Nathan, 116
master data update MEIO applications, 72–5
Materials Requirements Planning (MRP), 31, 33, 40, 47, 63, 89, 127–8, 129–30, 133–4, 136–7, 165–70, 174
mathematical optimization, 15–16, 34
mathematics
    general optimization solvers and, 18–20
    inventory optimization and, 7–8, 15–16, 34, 37, 71, 770
    mathematical optimization and, 15–16, 34
    MEIO and, 2–3, 7–9, 37, 39–40, 63–4, 71, 77, 128, 134, 137, 166–7, 171–2
    multi-echelon planning and, 7–8, 37, 71
MathWorks, 18
MATLAB, 18–20
MCA Solutions, 8–9, 13, 21, 43, 47, 75, 150n3. *See also* Servigistics.
MEIO
    analytics and, 162–3
    basic function of, 7–13
    computational limitations and, 169–72
    cost optimization vs., 77–98

    cost/benefit estimation of, 139–41
    defined, 7–8, 127
    difference from other supply planning methods, 127–38, 165–70, 174
    history of development of, 165–74
    implementation of, 97–8, 138, 140–1
    inventory optimization and. *See separate entry.*
    inventory optimization-multi-echelon relationship in, 65–76
    model network of, 66–70
    multi-echelon planning and. *See separate entry.*
    resistance to, 142
    scope of, 8–9
    service level agreements and, 115–26
    simulation and, 46, 99–113, 161
    user interface of, 45, 75–6, 107–9, 113, 161–2
    See also multi-echelon planning, inventory optimization *and various subjects related to MEIO.*
METRIC, 171
Muckstadt, J.A., 116, 170
multi-echelon inventory optimization. *See* multi-echelon planning.
multi-echelon planning
    automotive service sector and, 50–2
    basics of, 7, 34, 37–9
    key features of, 45–7
    networks in, 40–3
    relation to inventory optimization, 39, 65–76
    safety stock and, 23
    sequential processing and, 132
    setting service level in, 52–62

supply chain precision in, 62
See also inventory optimization *and* MEIO.
multi-sourcing, 90–2

Navicat, 103
new business costs and, 106, 113, 125

Office of Naval Research, 170
operational maintenance, 134–5, 137
ordering strategies, synchronization of, 46
Orlicky, Joe, 167–8

parent and child locations, 11, 37–8, 40, 69
penalty costs. *See* implicit costs.
PlanetTogether, 111–12
planned procurement, 70–1
planning process, MEIO's value to, 43–4
Plossl, George, 30–1, 93–4, 167
precision of control, supply network, 62, 105–6, 113
product mix, service levels set at, 56
production orders, 70–1
production planning and scheduling, 10
product-location combination, service levels set at, 54
Project Air Force, 170

RAND Corporation, 169–72
ranking recommendations, 72–5
redeployment, 24, 69–70
regional distribution centers, multi-echelon networks and, 41–3, 46–8, 63
replenishment strategies, 43–4, 46

safety stock
    cost of violating, 77
    dynamic, 21–3, 31–2, 118
    facility capacity and, 24
    meaning of "optimization" of, 23, 34
    penalty costs and, 61, 83–4
    target stocking level optimization vs., 31–2, 34
sales and operations planning (S&OP) process, 106, 113
sales organizations, conflict with supply chain organization, 118–120, 122–4
SAP Supply Network Planner (SNP), 103–4, 130–1
SCM Focus, 46
segmentation, inventory optimization and, 32–3
sequential location planning, 44
sequential processing, 129–30, 132, 137
Servigistics, 45, 70, 73–5, 107, 109, 150. *See also* MCA Solutions.
service level
    configuration of, 119
    consumer of, 57–8
    control of, 31, 34–5, 117–18, 123
    cost optimization and, 83, 93
    differentiated, 46
    direct controls over, 31, 34–5
    hierarchy of, 16, 96–7, 105–6
    inventory and, 16, 25–31, 34–5, 58, 60, 67, 71–3, 76, 83, 94, 98, 109, 118
    making changes to, 59–60
    setting of, 52–60, 96–7
    target days of supply and, 61–2
service level agreements
    basics of, 115–16

    history of, 116–17
    MEIO and, 115–26
    new business costs and, 106, 113, 125
    pricing of, 120–1
    sales-supply chain organization relationship and, 120, 122–4
service parts networks, 43, 50
Shamir, Joseph, 129
Sherbrooke, Craig C., 3, 5, 170–1
simulation
    accuracy of, 110–11
    cost optimizers and, 101–2
    defined, 100–1, 113
    ease of use of applications, 102–3
    flexible data capability and, 104–5, 113
    general optimization solvers and, 17
    initial vs. post go-live, 111
    MEIO and, 46, 99–113, 161–2
    new business costs and, 106, 113
    precision of control in, 105–6, 113
    safety stock calculation and, 24
    sales and operations planning (S&OP) process and, 106, 113
    service level-inventory investment interaction and, 31, 35, 109–10
    strategic vs. online, 111–13
    user interface and, 107–9, 113, 161–2
single-echelon networks, 40–3
SKU levels, 32–3, 35
SmartOps, 8, 21, 27, 72, 150, 162
socialization of MEIO, 23, 81, 94, 98, 128, 140, 143,
software as solution (SaaS), 116

specialization, optimization. *See* customization of optimization.
stocking levels, service level and, 58
Structure Query Language (SQL), 103–5
Sun Microsystems, 119
supply planning, relationship of MEIO to, 7–13, 34
system maintenance, 134–6, 138

target days of supply, 60–2, 64, 118
target stocking level
    inventory optimization and, 21–2, 34
    safety stock and, 31–2, 34
TOAD, 103
ToolsGroup, 8–9, 45, 104–5, 109, 111, 129, 149
total stocking level, 31–2
transactional recommendation generating applications, 72–5

U.S. Government, software development and, 167, 174
user interface
    alerts and, 75–6
    effectiveness of, 107–9
    visibility and, 45, 107–9, 113, 161–2

Vigoroso, Mark, 150n3
visibility, 45, 107–9, 113, 161–2

Wallis, Richard, 111
Wight, Ollie, 167

CPSIA information can be obtained at www.ICGtesting.com
Printed in the USA
BVOW01s2315211014

371751BV00019B/512/P